Remembering Aizu

Remembering Aizu

*The Testament
of Shiba Gorō*

Edited by Ishimitsu Mahito

Translated, with Introduction & Notes, by
Teruko Craig

University of Hawai'i Press
Honolulu

Originally published as *Aru Meiji-jin no kiroku: Aizu-jin Shiba Gorō no isho* by Chuo koronsha, 1971
English translation ©1999 University of Hawai'i Press
All rights reserved
Printed in the United States of America
11 10 09 08 07 06 7 6 5 4 3 2

LIBRARY OF CONGRESS CATALOGING-IN-PUBLICATION DATA

Shiba, Gorō, 1860?–1945.
 [Aru Meijijin no kiroku. English]
 Remembering Aizu: the testament of Shiba Gorō/Shiba Gorō;
edited by Ishimitsu Mahito; translated, with introduction and
notes, by Teruko Craig.
 p. cm.
 Includes bibliographical references.
 ISBN 0-8248-2130-0 (alk. paper)
 ISBN-13: 978-0-8248-2157-9 (pbk. alk. paper)
 ISBN-10: 0-8248-2157-2 (pbk. alk. paper)
 1. Shiba, Gorō, 1860?–1945. 2. Generals—Japan—Biography.
I. Ishimitsu, Mahito, 1904–1975. II. Craig, Teruko. III. Title.
U55.S386A313 1999
355'.0092—dc21
[B] 99–10265
 CIP

Printed by The Maple-Vail Book Manufacturing Group
Book design by Deborah Hodgdon

www.uhpress.hawaii.edu

Contents

Acknowledgments

I owe many thanks. Haruko Iwasaki, Matsuzawa Hiroaki, Maeda Norihiro, and Noguchi Shin'ichi patiently answered my queries. Patricia Crosby expedited the publication process. I am particularly indebted to Shiba Yoshifumi, who kindly lent me Shiba Gorō's original manuscript, and to Shiba Keiko, who shared her knowledge of the Shiba family. My greatest debt is to Phyllis Birnbaum, who made suggestions on matters of style, and to my husband, Albert Craig, who gave me advice and encouragement throughout the project.

Introduction

History is often a chronicle of the winners. This is certainly true of the Meiji Restoration and the subsequent transformation of Japan during the second half of the nineteenth century. We know of Chōshū and Satsuma, the domains that carried out the Restoration, and of Ōkubo Toshimichi, Saigō Takamori, Kido Takayoshi, Itō Hirobumi, and others from those domains who went on to build modern Japan. Even today, these figures are revered in Japan as "the great men of Meiji."

Among the losers in the Restoration, the Aizu domain lost the most. For its loyal support of the Tokugawa house and its staunch opposition to the enemies of the *bakufu*, the shogun's government, Aizu was treated most harshly by the new Meiji rulers: Its lands were confiscated and its samurai population exiled to the Shimokita Peninsula, at the northernmost frontier of Honshu. Unprepared for the severe winters and inexperienced in farming, the Aizu samurai lived on the edge of starvation; many succumbed to illness and disease.

One of those sent to the far north was Shiba Gorō (1859–1945). During the siege of Aizu Castle, in 1868, his grandmother, mother, and two sisters committed suicide so the men in the family could do battle without distraction. His father, a high-ranking samurai, and four brothers fought in the war. One brother was killed early on, but the rest of the men survived—contrary to their expectations. Gorō, as a child of

ten, had been sent to the Aizu countryside, away from the fighting. After two years of privation and hardship in the north, Gorō became an attendant at a prefectural office and was then taken by a finance ministry official to Tokyo, where he obtained work as a servant. A year later, at the age of fifteen, he gained admission to the Army Cadet School and, after that, to the Officers Academy. He rose through the ranks, won international acclaim as the colonel in charge of Japanese forces in Peking during the Boxer Rebellion, and eventually became a full general, a singular distinction for an Aizu "samurai" in an army dominated by former samurai of the Chōshū domain.

This book is Shiba Gorō's own story of his early life and times. It is also the story of the Aizu domain and those of its samurai who survived the struggles of the Restoration era.

FOUNDING OF THE AIZU DOMAIN

After unifying all of Japan in 1600, Tokugawa Ieyasu had made three of his sons daimyo, giving them lands and retainers. These were the "three families," the most honored of the collateral houses. The second shogun, Tokugawa Hidetada, also wished to establish a son, his third, as a domain lord. The circumstances, however, were complicated, for the son was by a concubine, and the shogun had a jealous wife six years his senior. Hidetada secretly placed the infant, born in 1611, with a nun for safekeeping, and in 1617 gave the child for adoption to Hoshina Masamitsu, the daimyo of Takatō. Takatō was a 30,000-*koku* hereditary domain in central Japan.* Hidetada's

*During the Tokugawa period (1600–1868), there were three categories of daimyo. The *fudai*, or hereditary daimyo, were those who had been Tokugawa vassals before 1600. Their holdings were mostly small, but they staffed the governing councils within the *bakufu*. The *shinpan*, or collateral daimyo, were the children of early shogun who had been given fiefs. They usually had no formal role in the *bakufu*, though they sometimes gave advice. If the shogun was without a male heir, however, a collateral daimyo could be adopted and become shogun. The *tozama*, or outside daimyo, were lords who had become Tokugawa vassals after 1600. They ruled their own domains but had no role in *bakufu* governance. Under Tokugawa rule, all daimyo were obliged to spend alternate years in Edo (Tokyo), the shogunal capital.

wife died, and in 1629 the son, known as Hoshina Masayuki, was permitted to meet his real father, now retired as shogun, for the first time. He succeeded his adoptive father as daimyo of Takatō in 1631. Tokugawa Iemitsu, the son of Hidetada by his proper—and jealous—wife, became the third shogun in 1623. He made great efforts to establish a close relationship with his half brother Hoshina Masayuki. In 1636, he named Masayuki to be the daimyo of Yamagata, a domain of 200,000 *koku*, and in 1643, moved him to Aizu, a domain with an official assessment of 230,000 *koku*. He also bestowed on his half brother additional revenues of 53,000 *koku* from Minamiyama, an adjoining *bakufu* holding. The Aizu domain was a mountainous, landlocked region in central northeastern Japan. Its castle town of Wakamatsu was at the southern end of a small plain, situated at the juncture of five roads that spread out through northeastern Honshu. Aizu was, consequently, a holding of strategic importance as a buffer between the Tokugawa heartland to the southwest and more northerly outside domains.

Confident that he had the shogun's support, Masayuki set about establishing control over his new domain. The steps he took were not unlike those being taken in other domains at the time: He changed the fief rents collected by samurai fief holders to stipends paid by the domain government; he set aside reserves of rice and money for use in emergencies; he encouraged the production of rice and such handicrafts as lacquerware and candle wax; he forbade the sale of human beings and limited indentured apprenticeships to ten years. Signboards posted throughout Aizu proclaimed these and other measures.

Even while reforming Aizu, Masayuki's counsel was increasingly sought by the shogun Iemitsu. Masayuki served his half brother unstintingly, earning for himself and his descendants a permanent seat—one of four—in the *tamarinoma* chamber of Edo Castle, the chamber reserved for daimyo with an advisory role in *bakufu* affairs. (At this time Aizu was still classified as an outside domain. It was officially recognized as a collateral domain and permitted the use of the surname Matsu-

daira and the use of the shogunal hollyhock crest only in 1699.) In 1651, Masayuki was asked by the dying Iemitsu to serve as guardian for his ten-year-old heir, Ietsuna. In this capacity Masayuki acted as the de facto head of the *bakufu* during the first half of Ietsuna's rule.

While Masayuki's duties kept him in Edo, he did not neglect Aizu. In 1668, with the help of Confucian scholar Yamazaki Ansai, he drew up a house code to serve as a guide for his retainers. Several of its injunctions were moral:

> Do not neglect military readiness.
>
> Take as fundamental the way of the samurai.
>
> Do not confuse the duties of the higher and lower ranks.
>
> Older brothers should be respected and younger brothers loved.
>
> The words of women should be totally disregarded.
>
> Lawbreakers should not be treated with lenience.

A few items in the code dealt with particulars of government:

> Other than elders [*karō*, the highest-ranking retainers], no one should have a voice in determining punishments and rewards.
>
> If a retainer acts beyond his station, he should be dealt with strictly.
>
> The money and rice set aside for emergencies are to be used for the common people, and only in times of famine.

But by far the most important injunction was the first:

> Serve the shogun with single-minded devotion. Do not measure your loyalty by the standard of other domains. If any Aizu daimyo is disloyal to the Tokugawa house, he is no descendant of mine, and on no account are you to obey him.[1]

Throughout the Tokugawa period, at the beginning of each new year, the code was read aloud by the school magistrate in

the presence of the daimyo and assembled samurai, who listened with heads bowed.

AIZU, A TOKUGAWA DOMAIN

The story of Aizu after Masayuki's death, in 1672, paralleled that of other large northeastern domains. For several generations it prospered. The castle town became a commercial as well as political center. But beginning in the early eighteenth century, deteriorating finances led the government to raise taxes and borrow from Mitsui and other merchant houses. In 1720, villagers in Minamiyama rebelled in protest against high taxes and corvée labor. In 1749, following a series of poor harvests, hundreds of Aizu peasants smashed and looted the houses of moneylenders and merchants, and breached the walls of the upper samurai district just outside the castle. The rioting, which lasted for seven days, was the worst of its kind in Aizu during the Tokugawa period. Forced to lower taxes, the domain borrowed more heavily; by 1752, it owed 364,800 gold ryō. To stabilize its revenues, it shifted the tax base from yearly surveys of land yield to a several-year moving average.

Finances recovered somewhat thereafter until 1781, when Aizu, and the rest of Japan, suffered another series of bad harvests. These marked the beginning of the Tenmei famine, which was particularly severe in northeastern Japan. In Aizu, the price of rice soared, starvation and disease were rampant, and many villagers abandoned their land. After agriculture recovered somewhat in 1787, the fifth daimyo, Matsudaira Katanobu, initiated a domain reform in tandem with the Kansei reform by the *bakufu* leader Matsudaira Sadanobu. Villages were put under the direct control of district officials, land was divided more equitably, production of candle wax, sake, and other local products was encouraged to counter the excessive dependence on rice, and rewards and punishments were reformed. Posts in the government were opened to men of talent, but at the same time,

social status was reinforced: Each of the eleven ranks of samurai was distinguished by the color of the ribbons used to fasten their *haori* surcoats or by the color of their kimono collars.

A most notable feature of Aizu was the moral training it gave to samurai of rank. Boys from ages six to nine were organized into neighborhood play groups of ten (*asobi no jū*). They spent the morning studying with individual teachers and in the afternoon met by turn at each other's homes. Before their play began, the most senior of the group recited the "seven rules."

1. We must not disobey our elders.

2. We must always bow to our elders.

3. We must not lie.

4. We must not act in a cowardly manner.

5. We must not pick on those who are weaker.

6. We must not eat in public.

7. We must not talk to girls.[2]

As each rule was proclaimed, the boys would respond, "Yes, yes," with vigorous nods of their heads. At the end they chorused, "Those things that are forbidden, we must not do." Punishments for infractions of the rules were graded and ranged from a slap on the hand with a bamboo rod, to holding a hand briefly over an open fire, being buried briefly in snow, or ostracism from the group. Ostracism was the most serious punishment, and an apology by parents was required for readmission to the group.

From age ten, samurai boys attended schools; by the end of the eighteenth century, a variety of schools had been established for samurai of all ranks, and for commoners as well. As a part of the fifth daimyo's reforms, a domain school, the Nisshinkan, had been built for the education of the four highest ranks of samurai. It was completed in 1803, and in the same year, the "Nisshinkan Injunctions for Children," a textbook, was compiled for the instruction of entering students. The book contained passages from the *Classic of Filial Piety* and other Confucian works, stories of exemplary Japanese historical figures,

and detailed injunctions on proper comportment. One injunction—no doubt useful at the school—was not to yawn or look bored in front of one's elders. The school taught the Chinese classics, the Neo-Confucianism of Yamazaki Ansai, mathematics, medicine, astronomy, some Shinto studies, and the usual military subjects. The school grounds, located close to the castle, were extensive and contained a Confucian temple, two-storied lecture halls, a printing shop, a swimming pond, a teahouse, and even a rudimentary observatory. Aizu historians regard it as having been one of the finest schools in Japan at that time.

In 1805, a further set of seventeen rules was drawn up. Known as the "Instructions for the Very Young," it bid children to rise early, wash their hands, rinse their mouth, not to begin eating until their parents had picked up their chopsticks, and so on. Little was left to chance. The rules no doubt applied to samurai daughters, as well as to sons, though books about Aizu are uniformly silent on the subject of their education. Girls presumably learned their letters at home. One authority does mention, however, that mothers made their children rehearse ritual suicide (*seppuku*) in front of the household Buddhist altar and gave their daughters daggers as a part of their trousseaus.[3]

Every Tokugawa domain had institutions to educate and discipline its samurai, but historians of Aizu view that domain's samurai as having had an especially strict training. The consciousness of the domain's close ties to the Tokugawa house, the founder's injunction to serve it with unconditional loyalty, and the stress on hierarchy and self-discipline are seen as having shaped a distinctive ethos. Aizu samurai were known to be proud, austere, narrow-minded, and, above all, stubborn. Such was the character of the "Aizuppo."

AIZU IN THE MEIJI RESTORATION

In the years before Perry's arrival in 1853, Aizu, like other domains, was assigned the task of bolstering Japan's coastal defenses. Despite financial difficulties, the domain performed

its duties as commanded. In 1806, after Russian raids on settlements in Hokkaido, Aizu patrolled the island's northern coast for three months. In all, 1,200 troops, most of whom had never been to sea, participated in the action. Costs were defrayed by borrowing from Aizu merchants and by selling to commoners the right to bear surnames and swords. In 1810, Aizu was ordered to patrol the Miura Peninsula to the south of Edo. The 180 troops it sent remained for ten years, and to pay for their upkeep, samurai stipends in the domain were cut. In 1846, Aizu was told to patrol the coast of the Bōsō Peninsula, a strategic area to the southeast of Edo across "Tokyo" Bay. The cost of maintaining 230 troops for seven years was defrayed by a temporary grant of the income from *bakufu* lands assessed at 31,000 *koku*. In consequence, though Aizu was a landlocked domain removed from centers of culture, commerce, and political power, its government and a considerable portion of its ruling class were made aware of a potential foreign threat to Japan.

Perry opened Japan to diplomatic relations with the West in 1854. During the four years that followed, a few collateral and outside daimyo emerged to seek a voice in national policy-making. They challenged the power of the hereditary daimyo, who, as *bakufu* councilors, had determined such matters. But in this first phase of Restoration politics, Aizu had no role; its daimyo, Matsudaira Katamori (1835–1893), was too young. Born the sixth son of the daimyo of Takasu, a collateral domain of 30,000 *koku*, Katamori had been adopted in 1846 as the heir to the daimyo of Aizu. He succeeded his adoptive father in 1852, at age seventeen, just one year before Perry's first visit to Japan. A later photograph of Katamori shows a young man of delicate build with regular, finely honed features; though dressed in full military attire, his expression is tentative and not particularly warlike. He was nevertheless said to be "direct and soldierly," with a reputation for "gentle humility and integrity."[4]

Aizu was also inactive during the second phase of politics, from 1858 to 1860, when the hereditary daimyo councilors reestablished their control over national politics. Headed by Ii

Naosuke, they purged daimyo, nobles, and samurai who had
attempted to enter politics during the earlier period, decided the
shogunal succession in favor of their own weak candidate, and
signed a commercial treaty with the United States over the
objections of the Kyoto court. Their reimposition of authority
worked well until 1860, when Ii was assassinated by fanatics
from the Mito domain. Ii's successors lacked the determination
to continue his tough-minded policies, and the *bakufu* began to
drift.

A third phase of politics, from 1860 to 1863, saw the
Kyoto court emerge as an alternate center of political power.
Supporting the court were radical young samurai, whose slogan
was "Honor the emperor and expel the barbarians." Implied in
the slogan was a criticism of the *bakufu*, which had been unable
to expel the foreigners or deny them treaties and trade. Also
supporting the court was the Chōshū domain, which had been
more successful than Satsuma in mediating between the court
and the *bakufu*. By late 1862, this combination of Chōshū and
radical samurai held sway in Kyoto; together they plotted,
assassinated "enemies of the court," and disrupted the social
order. Parallel to these events during this third phase of politics
was the reemergence of moderate collateral and outside daimyo
who had been the targets of Ii's purge. They succeeded in tak-
ing national policy-making out of the hands of the *bakufu*
council and into their own. This was achieved when Tokugawa
Yoshinobu, daimyo of the Hitotsubashi house, was appointed
as regent to the young shogun, and Matsudaira Keiei (Yoshina-
ga; Shungaku), daimyo of Fukui, was named as supreme coun-
cilor (*seiji sōsai*).

It was at this point that Matsudaira Katamori of Aizu
stepped onto the stage of national politics. In 1862/5,* at the
age of twenty-seven, he was made a *bakufu* advisor (*san'yo*).
Several months later, he was named to the newly created post
of Kyoto protector (*shugoshoku*); as protector he would take
over from the Kyoto deputy (*shoshidai*) the vital tasks of pro-

*See p. 23 for translator's explanation of dates and calendar years.

tecting the security of the emperor and palace and policing the city of Kyoto. His appointment had been engineered by Yoshinobu and Keiei to strengthen their hand in Kyoto.

On hearing of Katamori's appointment, two Aizu elders hurried to Edo to advise him against accepting the post. Taking the position, they counseled, would be extremely risky—like "trying to put out a fire while carrying a load of firewood." Heeding their advice, Katamori declined the appointment on the grounds that he lacked the talent to perform so important a task. He also protested that his samurai were unfamiliar with the ways of the imperial capital. Yoshinobu and Keiei immediately joined in efforts to persuade Katamori to accept the position. Aizu, they argued, had proven its loyalty to the *bakufu* over the years, political opinion within the domain was united, and its samurai were renowned for their stern warrior deportment. In one of several letters he sent to Katamori, Keiei wrote that "were Hoshina Masayuki alive today, he would certainly take on the job."[5] Unable to resist such arguments, Katamori accepted the post in 1862/i8. He left Edo with a force of some one thousand Aizu samurai and arrived in Kyoto late in the year.*

With the arrival of Katamori, the tide that had favored Chōshū began to recede. Katamori asked for more troops to suppress extremist activity and wider authority to better control the daimyo and *bakufu* officials who had converged on the city. He quickly established contacts with pro-*bakufu* nobles, won the trust of the conservative emperor Kōmei, and began talks with representatives of Satsuma, who were disgruntled at Chōshū's success. The turning point came in 1863/8, when troops from Aizu and Satsuma seized the palace gates in a military coup d'état.[6] Then, having cut off Chōshū's access to the court, they speedily suppressed the radical pro-emperor samu-

*As Kyoto protector, he was given 50,000 *ryō* as an office salary (*yakuryō*), a loan of 30,000 *ryō* to cover travel costs to Kyoto, and a monthly allotment of two thousand bales of rice and rice revenues equivalent to 10,000 *ryō*. These generous emoluments, we imagine, helped persuade him to accept the job.

rai movement in Kyoto. As the chief policeman of Kyoto, it is not surprising that Katamori was particularly disliked by the young extremist samurai.[7]

The Satsuma-Aizu coup inaugurated a fourth phase of politics, from 1863/8 to 1866, in which national decision-making centered on Kyoto and was in the hands of Yoshinobu, Katamori, and, to a lesser extent, Matsudaira Sadaaki, who was Katamori's younger brother and the new Kyoto deputy. During these years, the fortunes of Chōshū continued to plummet. In 1864, its forts at Shimonoseki were captured and destroyed by a four-nation fleet in retaliation for its having fired on foreign ships. Later in the same year, Chōshū troops were defeated by Aizu and Satsuma forces when they tried to recapture the Kyoto Palace. In 1865, Chōshū was forced to surrender to a twenty-four-domain *bakufu* army. The severed heads of the domain elders responsible for its radical policies were forwarded to the *bakufu* army headquarters. Originally, Katamori had been ordered to command the *bakufu* army, but the order was countermanded when it was decided that his role in Kyoto was critical.

Aizu's fortunes were decisively reversed in the final phase of politics leading to the Meiji Restoration, from 1866 to 1868. A civil war in Chōshū returned the radicals to power in that domain. Satsuma withdrew from the Kyoto coalition and entered into a secret alliance with Chōshū; it felt that it had not been given a voice in politics commensurate with its role in the 1863/8 coup. A desperate Chōshū, armed with superior weapons, single-handedly defeated a second *bakufu* expedition in 1866. Katamori argued strongly that the expedition should reform and continue its attack, but it was called off when the shogun died in 1866/7. Yoshinobu became the new shogun a few months later. By then it was too late to restore the fortunes of the *bakufu*.

In 1867/12 (January 1868 by the Western calendar), Satsuma, in alliance with Chōshū, and with the support of several other domains, seized the Kyoto Palace and proclaimed

the restoration of imperial rule. As its first act, the new court government stripped the shogun of his lands and abolished all *bakufu* offices.

Yoshinobu had earlier offered to return the reins of government to the emperor, but his vision of imperial rule was of a council of daimyo, which he would control by reason of his vast lands. When it was announced that he would lose his lands, Yoshinobu, who had withdrawn to Osaka Castle, sent an army of 15,000 to recapture the court. Katamori's voice was one of the strongest in favor of this action; 1,600 Aizu troops joined the *bakufu* ranks. The *bakufu* army was defeated by the smaller but better-armed troops of Chōshū and Satsuma in a battle outside Kyoto. Two Satsuma participants later told Ernest Satow, a British legation interpreter, that the Aizu men "fought very bravely."[8] One samurai son remembers that his father deliberately disobeyed orders of retreat and charged with his sword into enemy ranks.[9] During the four days of battle, 120 Aizu samurai died and 158 were wounded.

When news of the battle's outcome reached Osaka, Yoshinobu, Katamori, and other *bakufu* leaders fled by ship for Edo. In Edo, Katamori argued that eastern Japan should unite in a war against the "traitors at the side of the throne." Yoshinobu, however, realized that such a war would be futile. He sent a letter of submission to the court and withdrew from Edo Castle to a temple to await the dispositions of the new government.

Katamori repaired to Aizu in 1868/2. Hoping to keep his lands and retainers, that is to say, hoping to be treated like other daimyo, he wrote to more than twenty daimyo asking them to intercede with the new government on his behalf. Katamori stated that he was willing to submit to the authority of the emperor's government, and protested that he had never opposed the court but had simply fought in self-defense against Satsuma and Chōshū and had wrongly been labeled "an enemy of the court." Not surprisingly, the Satsuma and Chōshū leaders in the new court government ignored his appeals and ordered the military subjugation of Aizu.

THE AIZU WAR

Early on, in 1868/1/17, the court government had ordered the Sendai domain to attack Aizu. Sendai did not comply. It was sympathetic to Aizu, and, like Aizu, saw the Restoration as a coup by a few western domains that had little national backing. In 1868/3, the government sent three thousand troops to Matsushima Bay, not far from the Sendai castle town, to put further pressure on the domain. If anything, the action backfired: Sendai joined the Yonezawa domain in convening a meeting of northeastern domains in 1868/4 and again in 1868/5. The outcome was a loose alliance of domains that protested the government's demands for Katamori's life and lands. Aizu and the other northeastern domains prepared for war.

The court government was not unhappy at the prospect of further military campaigns. It was confident that it could win the war and believed that victory would strengthen it against the domains in the rest of the country. By the spring of 1868, government armies had accepted the surrender of Edo and consolidated their grip on eastern Japan; by early summer they were advancing toward the northeast. The strategy of their commanders was to pick off the northeastern domains one by one. This was feasible because the alliance had no plan for joint military actions. Government troops followed the main trunk roads north and also landed on the coasts of the Sea of Japan and the Pacific Ocean. Several domains fought fiercely, but most surrendered quickly. The dates of surrender reveal the routes taken by the better-armed and numerically superior government forces: 7/29 Nagaoka, Nihonmatsu; 9/3 Yonezawa; 9/15 Sendai; 9/22 Aizu; and 9/23 Shōnai.

Of the battles in the northeast, that against Aizu was the most bitter. The government army originally planned to leave Aizu for last, for it was seen as the greatest and most determined foe. But in 1868/8 (late September by the Western calendar), Itagaki Taisuke, the field commander of one of the government armies, pressed for an immediate, full-scale attack against Aizu. "In this cold land," he said, "snow will inevitably

PRINCIPAL NORTHEASTERN DOMAINS

fall within thirty days, and a winter war will be disadvantageous for our troops who are accustomed to warmer climes." He added, "Aizu is the trunk and Sendai and Yonezawa are merely the branches and leaves. Once the trunk is destroyed, the branches and leaves will wither away."[10]

Most of Aizu's seven thousand troops, three thousand of whom were peasant recruits, were fighting beyond its borders to the south and northwest. Itagaki assembled three thousand troops, mainly from Chōshū and Satsuma, at the castle town of Nihonmatsu on the Ōshū trunk road to the east of Aizu. In a

ROUTE OF ITAGAKI'S TROOPS

brilliant tactical move, on 1868/8/21, he started out on a road that led southwest from Nihonmatsu, then took a mountain path northward and crossed the Bonari Pass into Aizu. His soldiers then seized a fortification at Inawashiro, a town to the north of the lake of that name, crossed a strategic bridge over the Nippashi River, entered Wakamatsu, and captured a northern gate in the outer wall of the castle on 8/23. Until arriving at the castle town, they met only the lightest resistance. They were marching on foot and carrying their own supplies, and so for that age, the two-day, thirty-seven mile advance from Nihonmatsu to the castle town was a lightning strike.

When Itagaki's troops attacked the northern gate, the domain authorities rang the fire bell to summon the elderly samurai men, women, and children to the protection of the castle. Earlier, when Katamori returned from Edo to the domain, he had exhorted his samurai to "fight to the death to wipe out the stain on Aizu's honor." The women and children had been told by the authorities that they were free to act as they saw fit. When the fire bell rang, men and women alike acted with a calm and determination that often crossed over into self-sacrifice; indeed, many seemed to embrace death. One wonders

X Shiba's house

▨ third enclosure

N

Yukawa River

WAKAMATSU CASTLE
The castle had two sets of defenses: an outer moat, with an earthen wall extending the length of its inner bank, and an inner moat, which surrounded the castle proper. The outer moat enclosed an area of about 534 acres and contained the residential quarters of the upper samurai—some 440 houses, the domain school, granary, stables, prison, and other structures. Of the sixteen gates in the wall, the one captured by Itagaki, as indicated by the arrow, was to the north.

if they saw their fortunes as so bound up with their domain that their world would end with its downfall. Or were their actions the consequence of the Aizu ethos of samurai duty and honor?

One samurai son, who was fourteen at the time, wrote afterward: "I hastened to the inner enclosure of the castle. I knew of course I would never return home . . . not that I had the time to think of such matters. . . . All the women in my family had resolved to die, and yet, as I took leave, not one person shed a tear."[11]

Many of the elderly, women, and children chose to stay at home, for as noncombatants they would only be a hindrance and needlessly consume provisions in the castle. Of those who stayed behind, 230 took their own lives. In Shiba Gorō's fami-

ly, his grandmother, mother, oldest brother's wife, and two sisters killed themselves. Elsewhere, another sister committed suicide with her wounded husband, two daughters, and two sets of her husband's parents, real and adoptive. In the family of Saigō Tanomo—the domain elder who had opposed Katamori's acceptance of the post of Kyoto protector—his mother, wife, five daughters, and two sisters killed themselves; if we include cousins and others in the extended family, twenty-one died in all. The older sister wrote as her farewell poem:

> Each time I die and am reborn in the world,
> I wish to return as a stalwart warrior.

The younger sister wrote:

> I have heard that this is the way of the warrior,
> and so I set out on the journey to the Land of the Dead.

Saigō's thirteen- and sixteen-year-old daughters composed a poem together:

> Hand in hand, we will not lose our way,
> So let us set forth on the mountain path to death.[12]

Another incident, famous in the annals of Aizu history, concerns the Byakkotai ("White Tigers"), a battalion of sixteen- and seventeen-year-old samurai youths who had been mustered to support the Aizu troops in battle. On 8/22, as Itagaki's troops advanced toward Wakamatsu, thirty-seven of the teenage soldiers were sent out with a larger force to halt the advancing troops. In the confusion of retreat, twenty became separated from the main body. They made their way to a hill, saw the castle shrouded in smoke, thought all was lost, and committed suicide. One survived.

Though Itagaki's troops had gained a foothold at a northern gate of the outer castle wall, other gates remained in Aizu hands. On hearing of the attack on the castle town, about one

thousand troops returned from defensive deployments on the domain's borders and entered the castle through a southern gate. Under cover of night, the Aizu men made forays into enemy positions. In one such foray, 110 of the raiders were killed. The corpses bore identification tags inscribed with their posthumous names and the phrase, "Died in battle on the twenty-ninth day of the eighth month, Keiō 4."

Reinforcements continued to bolster Itagaki's army until thirty thousand had assembled and surrounded the castle.[13] On 9/3, the Yonezawa domain surrendered and called on Aizu to cease its struggle. To this, the domain elder Sagawa Kanbei, who had fought at Toba-Fushimi outside Kyoto, replied:

> The reason we formed the alliance and took up arms was to remove the villains at the side of the emperor. Look at what their troops do: They plunder, kill innocent people, and rape—their cruelty knows no bounds. They are a band of evil men, not soldiers of the emperor. We have no recourse but to fight. I have heard that their commander-in-chief, Prince Ninnaji, has arrived at the village of Tōdera. . . . If I could meet with the prince and convince him that we are not enemies of the court, I would gladly submit. But without making this clear, I cannot possibly obey his order to surrender.[14]

On 1868/9/14, Itagaki launched an all-out offense: His troops burned the samurai houses in the outer castle precincts while fifty cannons pounded the castle day and night, some positioned 1,600 yards away on a hill overlooking the donjon. The Aizu warriors responded with old-fashioned, four-pound mortars with a trajectory of only eighty-five yards. Besieged within the inner walls of the castle were more than 3,000 warriors and more than 1,500 women and children. Women cooked and also nursed the wounded, older men molded bullets, and children flew kites in a vain demonstration of high morale. Soon ammunition, food, and water ran low; dead bodies were thrown into empty wells.

Katamori, having no choice but to surrender, asked Yonezawa to intercede. On the twenty-second of the ninth month, one

month after the siege had begun, a white flag was raised above the northern gateway of the castle. During the nine months between the battle outside Kyoto and the surrender of the castle, 2,610 Aizu men had died.[15]

AFTERMATH OF THE SURRENDER

Two days after the surrender, government troops entered the castle. Katamori was confined in a temple on the outskirts of Wakamatsu, and the men in the castle were sent to a camp in Inawashiro. One prisoner was a woman, Yamamoto Yaeko. Dressed in the clothes of her brother, who was killed in the battle outside Kyoto, she had insisted on being called by his name and fought side by side with the men. The men deployed at the domain borders were sent to a camp in Shiokawa. The elderly and women and children were free to do as they wished. In 1868/10, Katamori was sent to Tokyo; his death sentence was commuted to life-long domiciliary confinement.* The domain was confiscated. The following year, the Aizu samurai were sent to detention camps in Tokyo and in Takata on the Sea of Japan.

In 1869/11, Katamori's infant son was given permission to revive the daimyo name and line. He was granted land on the Shimokita Peninsula, at the northeastern tip of Honshu in what is now Aomori Prefecture. The new domain, named Tonami, consisted of two separate pieces of land composed mostly of volcanic ash and was buried half the year in snow. Tonami was assessed as having a product of thirty thousand *koku* of rice, but actually yielded less than one-fourth that amount. Late in the spring of 1870, the Aizu samurai in Tokyo and Takata left for Tonami. Their families in Aizu were allowed to join them soon after. The relocated population numbered about 14,800, or 2,797 samurai families.[16] Their rice stipends were miserably small. They knew nothing of farming, but attempted to farm marginal lands. Inade-

*The government ordered one of the surviving domain elders to commit ritual *seppuku*.

N

Mt. Osorezan ▲

Mt. Kamafuse ▲

Tanabu

Yokohama •

Mutsu Bay

Pacific Ocean

Arito •

Noheji •

Aomori •

TONAMI DOMAIN

quately sheltered and clothed, many fell victim to malnutrition and disease. The local villagers, who saw them eating wild plants and roots, called them "Aizu caterpillars."

With the abolition of the domains in 1871/7, the new domain became Tonami Prefecture and was soon merged with other small neighboring prefectures to become Aomori Prefecture. The Aizu samurai were told they could stay or return to Aizu. About two hundred families remained.

The people of Aizu never forgave the leaders of Chōshū and Satsuma. Other domains in the northeastern alliance had seen their lands reduced, but Aizu alone had been abolished and its samurai sent into exile. It is noteworthy that even today some natives of the Aizu Wakamatsu area bear an enmity toward Chōshū and Satsuma. Local historians of the former Aizu still refer to the Chōshū and Satsuma forces as the "western army" and not as the government army, the usual term. Shiba Gorō's story is a vivid testimony to the tragic events of those years.

A NOTE ON THE TEXT

It is not certain when Shiba Gorō wrote his memoirs. In the preface to the published version (Chūō kōronsha, 1971), the editor, Ishimitsu Mahito (1904–1975), writes that Shiba showed him the manuscript in 1942, during World War II, with a request to improve the style. Ishimitsu was a journalist by profession; his father, a graduate of the Army Cadet School, had been befriended by Shiba in his youth. He took the manuscript home, and on reading it, was "struck dumb" and "overcome with awe" by Shiba's story. He copied the manuscript with Shiba's permission, and over several visits, held extended conversations to fill in the details and clarify factual and chronological inconsistencies. On these occasions, he recalls, Shiba was often moved to tears. By the time Ishimitsu had finished his revisions, Shiba was in his eighties; his siblings were all dead, as were his wives (he married twice) and several of his grandchildren. On Japan's defeat in August 1945,

Shiba attempted suicide; he died of his wounds four months later. With permission from the Shiba family, Ishimitsu called the revised manuscript to the attention of the Chūō kōron publishing house. It was published in 1971 as *Aru Meiji-jin no kiroku: Aizu-jin Shiba Gorō no isho* (The chronicle of a certain Meiji person: The testament of Shiba Gorō, a native of Aizu). Since then the book, which includes an essay by Ishimitsu, has gone through thirty-three printings.

Shiba's original manuscript was believed to have been lost, but in the early 1990s, it was discovered by his grandson Shiba Yoshifumi while he was sorting through family papers. The manuscript is written with brush on thin rice paper and bound in Japanese style. Its title page merely reads "Boshin junnan kaikoroku" (A memoir of the sacrifices of the Boshin War).

The difference between Shiba's original manuscript, which I have read, and the published version consists mainly of the information that Ishimitsu wove in to provide a larger historical context. This was a valuable contribution, though he added his own, more recent interpretations of historical events. When the narrative shifts from the personal to the general, it is often a shift from Shiba to Ishimitsu. In footnotes, I indicate one or two such interpolations. Ishimitsu's narrative also occasionally leaps ahead of the story line; for the sake of clarity, whenever appropriate, I have taken the liberty of putting these materials in a more chronological order. Ishimitsu also seems to have amplified certain dialogues in the original manuscript, presumably based on his conversations with Shiba. Some original material has been omitted; usually it is of minor importance— lists of names, several rather artless poems, an account of an excursion to Kamakura and Mount Fuji with friends. The one serious, and to me inexplicable, omission is Shiba's account of the neighborhood association of young boys to which, he says, he owed his lifelong habits of self-reliance. I have restored this passage to the text, suitably footnoted. The prose style of Shiba and Ishimitsu, apart from occasional literary flourishes by the

latter, is very much the same—the sober classical style (*bungo-tai*) favored by those educated during the early Meiji era. The chapter titles were added by Ishimitsu. Footnotes and information enclosed in square brackets are the translator's.

TECHNICAL INFORMATION

In both the introduction and translation, I have used the dates given in the published text. These follow the Japanese lunar-solar calendar up to the time the Western calendar was adopted, on January 1, 1873. Thus, for simplicity's sake, in the introduction, I write 1868/8/22, instead of writing "the twenty-second day of the eighth month of 1868." Needless to say, the year 1868 in the Western solar calendar is not exactly congruent with the generally equivalent year-period in the lunar-solar calendar; depending on the date, it would be more precise to say Keiō 4, or Meiji 1. Every few years the lunar-solar calendar required the insertion of an extra, intercalary month. This is indicated as follows: 1862/i8. In the translation itself, I have used such phrases as "the twenty-second day of the eighth month" to retain the flavor of the Japanese text. Wherever relevant, I have provided the Western calendrical equivalent.

I have also left ages in the Japanese count, by which reckoning a child is one on the day of his birth and two on New Year's Day of the next calendrical year. Shiba, who was born in 1859/5/3, would have been a little over nine years and four months old at the time of the siege in 1868, an intercalary year. In Japanese usage, the family name comes first. When I have been unable to ascertain the reading of a name, or when Japanese sources differ, I have chosen the most commonly accepted reading. I have also amended several incorrect transcriptions of proper names that appear in the published edition.

Gold was the basis of coinage in eastern Japan, where Shiba lived. The standard unit was the *ryō*. One *ryō* equaled four *bu*, or sixteen *shu*. Silver was the basis of coinage in western Japan.

The exchange rate between gold and silver remained fairly stable throughout the Tokugawa period, with one gold *ryō* equaling sixty silver *monme*. In the 1860s, however, silver began to decline, and by 1871, one *ryō* equaled 192 *monme*. Copper pennies, or *mon*, were used throughout the country. Copper was also steadily devalued, and in 1867, one *ryō* equaled about eight thousand *mon*. Under the New Coinage Act of 1871, the yen replaced the *ryō* as the basic unit. One yen equals one hundred sen or one thousand *rin*. In 1872, when Shiba went to Tokyo as a servant, one *shō* (1.805 liters) of rice cost about four sen. One could go to the public bathhouse for one sen five *rin*, or get a haircut, including a shave, for twenty-five sen. An English-Japanese dictionary cost two yen fifty sen. In 1875, one could buy a bowl of buckwheat noodles for eight *rin*, a bowl of *azuki*-bean soup for three sen, a sweet bun for five *rin*. A policeman's starting monthly salary was six to seven *yen*. The reader will note that Shiba refers to various denominations throughout the narrative.

The size of a domain was expressed in terms of its estimated annual rice yield as measured in *koku* of rice (one *koku* equals 5.1 U.S. bushels). A samurai's rank stipend, or the yearly amount of rice to which he was entitled, was also expressed in terms of *koku*.

Remembering Aizu

*The Testament
of Shiba Gorō*

Preface

I have often taken up my brush to write this account, but each time tears overwhelmed me, and I could not continue. Now I have reached my eighties with nothing to show for the years that have passed.

I retired to my humble dwelling near the River Tama quite a while ago and since then have rarely left to go to the city. I have enough simple clothes to cover my aging body and enough simple fare to sustain me for the remainder of my days. For this I am thankful. Yet when I cast my thoughts to the past, to Aizu, the land of my birth, its mountains and rivers, my spirit is troubled. I tell myself that this is just an infirmity of old age, but still I shed many fresh tears and feel unbearable sorrow and anguish.

My father, mother, brothers, and sisters have all been laid to rest; I alone am left in this world. Though I speak, no one answers. Though I cry out in grief, no one consoles me. The seasons bring their round of soft breezes and bright moons, snow and flowers; close by, the river glances through the leafy trees. And still, the dear faces of my grandmother, mother, and sisters, who came to such a violent end, rise up before me, as if to beckon me, to say they miss me, pity me—a weak and lonely old man.

The years have passed, and the villains and evildoers from Satsuma and Chōshū have long been consigned to their graves.

More lamentations will serve no purpose, nor is there any point in dredging up an ancient grudge. It is not rancor or anger that I feel, but rather an immense sense of loss and regret. This prevents me from attaining true wisdom and peace of mind.

How swiftly time flows! More than seventy years have passed since I was a child of ten living in Aizu. The *bakufu* had already returned its ruling power to the emperor, and our lord, who relinquished his post as Kyoto protector, had returned to Aizu to live in seclusion. A new age had peacefully dawned, or so my elders told me, but then, for reasons beyond my childish comprehension, Aizu was branded an enemy of the court—a rebel domain—and the entire populace was subjected to unspeakable abuses. The memory haunts me still.

I happened to be visiting my uncle's house in the countryside when I heard that Satsuma and Chōshū troops had stormed the outer defenses of Aizu Castle. Immediately, I thrust my dagger into my belt. Pushing my way through the fleeing crowd, I ran in the pouring rain to the pass near Kitaoyama Village. I looked for the castle, but it was engulfed in black smoke, and the city had become a raging sea of fire. All around, the air resounded with the deafening roar of gunfire. "Where are you going?" someone asked; "where is your family, young sir? Look, the whole city is on fire—there's no way you can enter the castle precincts. You'd better turn back." Others in the crowd urged me not to go on. I realized that I would not be able to reach my grandmother, mother, and sisters. I did not know then that they had already died by their own hand. I threw myself down on the roadside, beat the ground with my fists, tore at the grass, and wept aloud. All this I remember as though it happened yesterday.

The domain surrendered; I was taken captive with other samurai, and we were eventually sent to the Shimokita Peninsula in the far north. The domain had been transferred to that wasteland of volcanic ash. There, with only the clothes on our backs, barely enough to eat, no quilts to sleep on, and no hoes to till the soil, we lived in conditions worse than a beggar's. For food, we dug the roots of wild plants. We protected ourselves

from the freezing winds by hanging mats of rough straw in our huts. We survived months and years of hardship and privation, but our sufferings have been lost to the annals of history, and few people know about what we endured.

At times, my love and longing for my dead grandmother, parents, and sisters are almost too much to bear, and thus, with the great pain and anguish that still tears my heart, I dedicate this humble account to their memory.

Childhood

My father, Shiba Satazō, was a samurai of the Aizu domain. He belonged to the second highest stratum of upper samurai, the *kurohimo*, who fastened their *haori* surcoats with black ribbons and were entitled to wear ceremonial garments at all times. As such, he had the right to appeal directly to the domain elders and could bear a banner with his own insignia in battle. He held the office of captain (*monogashira*) in the domain military and received a yearly rank stipend of 280 *koku*.[1] I understand that he served with distinction under the battalion commander and that he was an influential presence in the domain.

My father was devoted to his children and loved them deeply, but, as was the custom of the time, he did not allow himself any informality in their presence. To a timid child like me, he seemed forbiddingly stern, and out of fear as much as deference, I kept my distance. Once in a while, he would pick me up and sit at the hearth with me on his lap. My entire body would stiffen with tension, and I would be unable to respond to his gentle questioning. At such times, I would secretly wish that he would let go of me.

My grandmother Tsune was then eighty and in excellent health. My mother, Fuji, was originally from the Hinata family. I had many siblings: my older brothers Taichirō (childhood name Hideharu), Kensuke (Shigeru), Gosaburō, and Shirō (Shigeshirō, literary name Tōkai Sanshi and author of *Chance*

Meetings with Beautiful Women), my older sisters Kayo (married into the Kimura family), Tsuma (married into the Mochizuki family), Shun (died in infancy), Soi (married into the Tsuchiya family), Iyo (died in infancy), and my younger sister, Satsu. [I was the second youngest.] The family was large, but, as the children were strictly brought up, the house was never noisy.

I was born in a house on Hon Sannochō, a street in the residential quarter for high-ranking samurai. We moved shortly after to Hon Ninochō, a street still closer to the castle. Years later, when a barrack for the Twenty-Ninth Infantry Division was built in the area, I had an earthen mound built to mark the site where my family committed suicide. Some time later, I planted a Himalayan cedar in their memory.

The family, as I said, was large. Several servants also lived with us, and because my mother had many duties and obligations as a samurai wife, she could not always attend to the needs of the children. So, in accord with the prevailing practice, soon after my birth, I was sent to live with a wet nurse, who was the wife of Sawada Jisuke. He was the head of a foot-soldier unit and lived in the northwest section of Wakamatsu. I stayed with the family for about three years, but to my great shame, I cannot recall the name of the woman who nursed me. After I was seven or eight and allowed to walk about on my own, I visited the Sawada family regularly once a month to pay my respects. Years later, I learned that Sawada died in the Boshin War.

Except for Shirō, my brothers were much older, and by the time I became fully aware of my surroundings, they were already in service at the domain office in Edo or in Kyoto. I seldom saw them and spent most of my days in the company of Shirō and my older sister Soi. I have forgotten the exact date, but one morning my sister Soi was as usual arranging my hair when I started to fret and complain about something. My mother overheard us quarreling and reprimanded my sister, ordering her to give back the new set of kimono she had recent-

ly received as a reward for good behavior. To this day, I can see my sister making her apologies and returning the clothes to my mother. The memory fills me with remorse. The quarrel had actually been my fault, and I was ashamed that I had not acknowledged this even though I was then still a child.

Strict by nature, my mother was admired as a wise and capable samurai wife. My knowledge of manners I chiefly owe to her. But she was also kind and affectionate. Sitting me on her lap, she would tell me the story of Momotarō and other children's tales, or she would recite over and over the poems from the *One Hundred Poets' Anthology,* or the famous lines in the *Taiheiki* about the warrior Toshimoto losing his way in the blizzard of cherry blossoms. As I recall, she did this with genuine pleasure. She also told me the story about the loyal warriors Kusunoki Masashige and his son Masatsura and the stories from China about the Twenty-Four Paragons of Filial Virtue. I still remember some of the passages, and whenever I recite them, I seem to feel the warmth of my mother's lap and can scarcely contain my yearning for her.

It must have been much the same in other domains, but in Aizu, the three-hundred-year-old Tokugawa feudal order regulated every aspect of our lives and every organization, both public and private. But as children, we did not feel particularly constrained, and this, I assume, was because we had been educated from childhood to conform to the practices of the society around us.

I mentioned that my father belonged to the *kurohimo* rank of samurai and always wore ceremonial clothes. His immediate superiors in the domain military, the *bangashira* and *shinbangashira,* belonged to the highest-ranking group—the *nandohimo*—and used *haori* ribbons of a grayish blue color. Below the *kurohimo* came two groups distinguished by their dark blue and light blue ribbons. The samurai in the top four strata were considered upper samurai. Beneath these were three groups distinguished, in descending order, by their light brown, yellowish green, and pale yellow *haori* ribbons. Last came the men col-

lectively known as the *erisei*, who wore kimono collars of black, persimmon, pale gray, or light yellow. There were all together eleven ranks of samurai, each identifiable at a glance by the color of their clothes.

A child could enter the Nisshinkan at age ten, and so at seven, I began taking private lessons with Sakurai Gorō and Iida Bunji, two teachers who lived in the neighborhood. We read the Confucian classics, which I found extremely boring, since we only memorized passages. No one explained their meaning. My only happy memory of the lessons was being given a baby carp by Sakurai-sensei.

I spent my afternoons with a neighborhood group of young boys called the *asobi no jū*. I owe a great deal to this institution. The spiritual training I received in the company of my peers served me well in the difficult years that followed. Indeed, in many ways, I feel I owe my very survival to the values and habits I absorbed unconsciously as a member of that group. I cannot praise it enough. We took turns playing at each other's houses but also spent time outdoors. In the spring and autumn, we often climbed a hill at Keizan Village and slid down the pine-covered slope while seated on a straw rice bag. In the summer, we splashed about in the Yukawa River or occasionally bathed in the hot springs at Tenneiji.*

As a child I had a peculiar weakness, which caused the family much worry. Fear would overcome me, and I would burst out crying the moment I saw anyone with a bald head. One New Year's Day—I must have been four or five—I was out in the field flying kites with my brother Shirō and several young men who were in my father's service. A priest from Erinji, our family temple, walked up approaching from behind. He suddenly picked me up and said, "Well, well, young master, I see you know how to fly a kite." He meant to be friendly, but I had been completely absorbed in flying my kite. Taken by surprise, I ran shrieking all the way home. From that time on, the sight

*I have combined two separate passages from Shiba's manuscript (unpaginated), which Ishimitsu, for some reason, omitted.

of a bald head filled me with fear and loathing; the mere thought was enough to give me gooseflesh.

I was afraid not only of shaven-headed priests but of old men who had lost their hair, not to mention blind musicians and masseurs.* One day, I was walking on the street when I noticed that an old man called Takemura was following a few steps behind. He was bald, and as usual, I started for home as fast as I could but tripped on a stone and fell. Then, just as the old man caught up with me, I saw a little topknot at the back of his head and immediately stopped crying.

My mother worried about this strange phobia of mine, and to help me get over it, she sent me away to relatives whenever a doctor, priest, or masseur was expected at the house. All to no avail. The habit persisted until I was well over six or seven, and she told me later that even the sound of a samisen† would remind me of a blind musician and would send me into a fit of crying. I regret causing my mother such worries, though now the memory brings a smile to my lips.

I was nervous and high-strung but otherwise had no ailments and grew up a healthy, well-behaved child. So well-behaved, in fact, that my mother, who doted on me, called me Kinnen [recent years] Gorō. This was because she said that she had not seen such a good child in recent years. But to be truthful, I was really a sissy and a coward. I disliked games that had anything to do with physical strength, invariably lost in sumo matches, and was not even once scolded for being naughty.

Yet even sissies came under the iron discipline of the domain. No matter how cold it was, I was not allowed to tuck my hands into the front of my kimono, and no matter how hot it was, I could not use a fan or strip to the waist. On meeting an older person on the street, I had to give way. When entering a house, I had to be careful not to step on the threshold, and once inside a room, I had to avoid walking in the middle. Also,

*People who had lost their sight often earned their living as wandering musicians and masseurs. They generally shaved their heads or wore their hair cropped short.

†A samisen is a three-stringed instrument plucked with a plectrum.

when guests came, I was not permitted to scold someone in their presence, not even cats or dogs, to say nothing of servants. Belching, sneezing, or yawning in front of others was forbidden. Nor was I ever to look bored. In sum, I—and all samurai children—had to submit to a strict code of etiquette.

Lately, I have heard that when people speak of samurai, they think of ruffians who bellow at the slightest provocation, get drunk, turn violent, and cut down commoners at will. They could not be more mistaken. Such men are really *rōnin*—masterless samurai who have gone to seed, or gamblers and their ilk, and do not represent samurai in general.

We also had to observe strict rules about money; we were forbidden to handle it. Just once a year, at the midsummer festival of the local Suwa Shrine, I would be given permission to buy sweet dumplings or some other snack, but even then, I would hand my pouch to the vendor and let him take out the appropriate sum. If I remember, a box containing six dumplings cost four *mon*, a peashooter and papier-mâché mask, ten *mon*, respectively.

Beginning
of the Tragedy

All was calm and peaceful in the years when I grew from a child of seven to ten, with nothing to suggest the catastrophe that would soon befall us. Naturally, as a child, I knew nothing of such matters as the financial troubles in other domains, the increasing numbers of samurai who abandoned their domains to engage in political violence, or the importunate demands by foreign powers to open the country's ports for trade. I spent each day close to my father and mother, and strict though they were, I grew up like a fledgling secure in the warmth of its parental wings.

But in the thirty or forty years before my birth in Ansei 6 [1859], the country had been beset by periodic famines, peasant uprisings, *rōnin* disturbances, and repeated threats and even acts of aggression by Western nations. I occasionally heard my brother Taichirō talking to my father during his visits home from Edo, but these matters were too complicated for me to understand. My father, moreover, was a man of few words, who kept his own counsel and avoided gossip of any kind. Taichirō would draw me aside now and then to try to explain what was happening, but on seeing my puzzled expression, he would cut the conversation short and say, "You'll understand in time. Right now, just concentrate on your studies."

In fact, the structure of society itself was changing rapidly. As the domains struggled to get by on agricultural revenues,

they could no longer meet expenses without the support of powerful merchants and moneylenders. Such merchants were given the right to wear swords and were elevated to samurai status. Even while simultaneously issuing stronger edicts about frugality, the domains went to great lengths to buy new Western weapons. The cost of living soared, the dissatisfaction of lower samurai gradually increased, and many quit their domains and fomented trouble in society.

To add to these woes, the Western powers were expanding in East Asia: Russia from the north, England and France from the west, the United States from the east. One after another, they sent gunboats and demanded the opening of ports. Their merchant ships entered ports unlawfully and caused terror and confusion. In the aftermath of China's defeat in the Opium War, these Western powers pushed forward with their quest for colonies, like frenzied wolves fighting over a carcass.

The leaders of the *bakufu* and domains were deeply concerned. Scholars at the *bakufu* Institute for Western Learning (Yōgakusho) judged that it was no longer possible to maintain national security under the policy of seclusion, and in the Ansei era [1854–1860], treaties of friendship were signed and ports opened to trade. Knowledgeable men in the domains understood the situation, but low-ranking extremist samurai opposed the *bakufu*'s actions. Distorting the true meaning of the slogan "Honor the emperor and expel the barbarian," they murdered foreigners and agitated against the opening of the country. The *bakufu* saw that it would not be able to expel the foreigners if the existing feudal structure continued, but efforts to establish a unified political structure failed, for the domains clung to the status quo and were unwilling to join in a common effort.

In the meantime, certain nobles at the Kyoto court conspired with extremist samurai. [In 1862], Katamori was appointed to the important post of Kyoto protector to keep the peace of the city. For almost six years he labored tirelessly, gathering information on *rōnin* activity and striving to maintain law and order. In spite of this, the turmoil did not cease. Furthermore, out of their excessive concern for the country, some of

our own samurai—retainers of the leading collateral domain, which had served the *bakufu* with unswerving loyalty in political and military affairs—had taken up the extremist cause and begun to plot in secret.* But all this, I learned years later.

In the first year of Keiō [1865], when I was seven, there were reports of a disturbance led by a band of Mito *rōnin* in the Nikkō area of Kōzuke Province. My father was sent to Nikkōguchi to defend the southern Aizu border. I still remember the stir and commotion when the soldiers under his command gathered at our house to make preparations. My father finished his duties before long, and on the day of his return, Shirō and I stood outside in the pelting rain to welcome him home.

Two years later, in Keiō 3 [1867], many of the men who were posted in Edo returned to Aizu. Samurai from other domains also came and were billeted at temples and samurai houses. My friends and I watched each day as the men drilled at the parade ground in the third enclosure of the castle. After they had finished, they let us have our own little drill practice.

The same year, on the fourth day of the tenth month, Shogun Tokugawa Yoshinobu decided to return the governing powers of his office to the emperor. The Aizu daimyo praised his courageous decision and led the others in expressing his support. On the twelfth, Yoshinobu called a meeting of his senior councilors and members of the inspectorate in order to hear their views. The majority supported his decision, but three shogunal advisors, Buzen-no-kami, Harima-no-kami, and Tango-no-kami, raised objections and warned him of a possible insurrection by samurai from Satsuma and Chōshū. Nevertheless, on the fourteenth, Yoshinobu formally notified the court of his intention. The next day, he and Katamori were summoned before the emperor. They were thanked for the faithful service rendered by both houses over the generations, and were told that while Yoshinobu's offer was accepted, in view of the

*This and the preceding three paragraphs, which are not in the original manuscript, illustrate the kind of insertion Ishimitsu made to provide a historical context.

world situation, all concerned should work as one to preserve the nation and put the imperial mind at ease.

But as was revealed later, on the fourteenth, one day before the imperial audience, Saigō Takamori and Ōkubo Toshimichi of Satsuma, the court noble Iwakura Tomomi and several other nobles and samurai had secretly obtained a banner and an imperial edict ordering Chōshū and Satsuma to kill Yoshinobu and punish Aizu by military force. The edict was dated the thirteenth. In the years to follow, the authenticity of both the banner and edict was called into question. I, of course, do not know the truth of the matter.[2]

Reaction in Aizu

The new year dawned. On the twenty-second day of the second month of Keiō 4 [1868], Katamori returned to Aizu. Reluctant to live in the castle, he went into seclusion at a residence nearby.

From ancient times, it has been known that it is better to attack than to defend. Yet, since the shogun's surrender of governmental powers Katamori had kept strictly away from any and all aggressive acts. In his wish to secure peace and avoid any conflict that might bring harm to the people, he silenced those who called for action and counseled patience and forbearance. Unfortunately, this only allowed Satsuma and Chōshū to drive Aizu farther into a corner.

On the twenty-seventh, Katamori issued a decree to the domain samurai. "The recent unfavorable turn of events is ultimately due to my incompetence. In allowing this to happen, I have disgraced myself completely. I daresay that you, too, find this turn of events most regrettable. I should tell you that while in Edo, I had hoped to take immediate action that would redress the situation. But the shogun was occupied with his own affairs, and so I decided to return to Aizu for the time being. We have now been told that the government has ordered several domains to punish Aizu with military force. If their troops advance to our borders, we have no choice but to make full preparations for war. I therefore entreat you to unite as one,

cast aside any doubts you may have, and do your utmost to vindicate the honor of our domain."

The decree was received by one and all with "gnashing of teeth and clenching of fists." What had been rumor was now confirmed, and as cries of sorrow and indignation filled the air, the whole castle town seemed to have gone into mourning. Even the children were enraged. I remember venting my anger by whacking my wooden sword against trees and bushes. "Take that, you good-for-nothing potato samurai! Come on— I'll show you a thing or two!" I whacked away until dark, the tears streaming down my face, and still I would not be calmed. At supper, no one uttered a word. "Potato samurai" was what we contemptuously called the Satsuma men, since we knew the people of Satsuma, too poor to eat rice, lived on a diet of sweet potatoes [Satsuma-imo]. The army organized against the *baku-fu* and Aizu was composed of troops from Satsuma, Chōshū, Aki, Tosa, and Ōgaki, but we singled out Satsuma, the leader, as our particular enemy.

From that day forward, Aizu changed completely. At home, my parents, brothers, and sisters said little and went about with lips tightly clenched and eyes flashing. My father, who had already retired, reported to the castle every day. My aunts and uncles and other relatives came by frequently to hold discussions in hushed tones. Even the servants whispered to one another in the corner.

It was the third month, and we welcomed the first signs of spring despite the threat of war. The familiar song of the bush warbler, the rivulets of melting snow, the new leaves glistening in the sun—all was the same. On the third, I joined my mother and sisters in celebrating the Festival of the Dolls; it was to be the last time. We set up the dais to display the dolls, draped a cloth of red felt over it, and lined up the brightly costumed emperor and empress, the three ladies-in-waiting, and the five court musicians. We then lit the miniature paper lanterns and arranged sprays of peach buds that had not yet fully matured. The scene remains fresh in my mind.

I asked my mother, "I was told the doll of the emperor rep-

resents His Majesty. Is this true?" In reply, she merely gazed
into my eyes and nodded. This year, too, as in the past, we had
displayed the doll of the emperor in his honor. So why were we
being called the enemy of the court, a rebel domain deserving
of punishment? It seemed to me unreasonable and unjust. I
could not suppress my indignation and turned to my mother for
an explanation, but when I saw the grim look on her face, I
decided not to pursue the matter.

For a child, it was most perplexing. My understanding was
that the shogun had carefully considered the situation and, as a
result, had returned his ruling powers to the emperor, resigned
from his official posts, and withdrawn from Edo to his ances-
tral home [in Mito]. Moreover, to avoid a military confronta-
tion, he had repeatedly sent messages expressing his submission
to the court. But his appeals had been ignored because the
samurai from Satsuma and Chōshū were plotting with nobles
to use the young emperor to dominate the new government.
And through all this, Aizu, which had long been entrusted with
the peace of Kyoto, had refrained from speaking out on any
issue pertaining to the court and had looked on in silence while
Satsuma and Chōshū went forward with their schemes.

I was now ten years old and ready to enter the Nisshinkan.
Taichirō, who was back from Edo on business, kindly made the
necessary arrangements and took me to the houses of school
officials and teachers for the usual courtesy calls. I was placed
in the Sanraijuku, the lower division of the school. We began
with the Confucian classics, but having read them since I was
seven, I learned nothing particularly new. The Sanraijuku was
the school for the children of upper samurai who lived near the
castle. The other three schools in the lower division were the
Mōshijuku, Gokyōjuku, and Shōshojuku.

I often saw Taichirō talking to my father in private. They
said nothing to the younger children, however, and my grand-
mother and mother also kept their thoughts to themselves.

My sister Soi presently came home from Edo. Only the year
before, when she was eighteen, she had married Tsuchiya Taka-
haru in Edo, but her husband had been sent to Kyoto soon

after. Several days after her return, we received word that he had died in the battle of Toba-Fushimi, outside Kyoto. My sister occasionally took me with her to visit her husband's grave. Even now, so many years later, my heart aches with sadness when I recall my sister offering flowers and prayers, her shoulders bent over with grief.

Summer came, and tension mounted as the enemy drew near and rumors circulated of troops running wild. The surrounding mountains seemed to echo with distant thunder, but if you listened closely, you could tell it was the sound of cannon fire rumbling across the skies. Danger was imminent, and though my father and Taichirō still said nothing, news of the fighting inevitably reached the children's ears, making us fume and rage. According to one rumor, *rōnin* from Satsuma and Chōshū were setting fires and murdering people in Edo and other places to stir up unrest, bring further dishonor to the Tokugawa, and foment hatred of Aizu. According to another rumor, the enemy troops left in their wake the corpses not only of soldiers but also of innocent townsmen, peasants, women, and children.

At home, my sisters began rising early to practice with their wooden halberds. With white bands tied around their hair and kimono sleeves tucked up, they drilled each day in the garden, shouting with each thrust of the halberd. I can still hear their voices, sharp and clear in the morning air.

The Nisshinkan was closed down and converted into a hospital. The dead and wounded were carried in day after day, and because there was a shortage of space, many had to be placed with families in the samurai quarters. The castle town had become a battlefield.

A Fight to the Death

For Aizu, it was no longer a question of preparing for war but of defending itself against attack. In war, the offensive side does not have an easy time but is nonetheless always at an advantage over the defensive side. The men in the domain were aware of this as they took up their positions and resolved to fight to the bitter end. Even so, there seems to have been a lingering hope that the castle, at least, might be spared and some manner of truce effected.

The fighting force was organized into four battalions, each named after a god traditionally believed to guard one of the four compass directions:

Seiryūtai (East): Men from ages thirty-six to forty-nine, who were responsible for the defense of domain borders.

Byakkotai (West): Youths from sixteen to seventeen, constituting a reserve force.

Shujakutai (South): Men from eighteen to thirty-five, who would engage in actual combat.

Genmutai (North): Men fifty and over, who were charged with the defense of the castle.

Some historians who have written about the war have portrayed Aizu as the ringleader of those who wanted to preserve the feudal order at any cost. These historians have seen Satsuma and Chōshū as the forces of liberation; supposedly,

Aizu peasants and townsmen welcomed them and even gave them their active cooperation. This is a gross distortion of the facts. There are countless documents that attest to the atrocities the enemy perpetrated on these very people, or for that matter, on common people throughout the northeastern domains. To my deep regret, these accounts have all been deliberately suppressed.

Four battalions were deemed inadequate for the defense of Aizu, and the domain decided to recruit commoners. A great many people responded, and although such loyalty was to be expected after long years of feudal rule, the threat of impending enemy attack undoubtedly acted as a further incentive. The peasant recruits, who ranged from ages twenty to forty, numbered 2,700. Supervising them were some 380 samurai—regional intendants and their subordinates. Smaller units were also formed: the Rikishitai, made up of sumo wrestlers and other men known for their physical prowess; the Shugentai, made up of itinerant monks and ascetics; the Ryōshitai, who were hunters; and the Kishōtai, who were Buddhist priests. Some recruits were later elevated to samurai status. In recruiting, there was no element of coercion; the men had been told beforehand that they were free to leave and seek shelter with relatives.

Taichirō was named a military commissioner and sent to the Echigo front, beyond the western border of the domain. My second oldest brother, Kensuke, was assigned to the artillery and sent to the Nikkō-Utsunomiya front to fight under the domain elder Yamakawa Ōkura. Soon after, we received news that he had disappeared while scouting the enemy position. My mother set up a little shrine inside a closet so that no one would see her when she prayed for the repose of his soul with offerings of food, flowers, and incense. (It was confirmed later that my brother had been captured near Tochigi.)* Gosaburō, my third oldest brother, was initially assigned to Sagawa Kanbei's unit but subsequently was made the leader of a peasant unit

*Kensuke was later mistakenly killed by Aizu peasants.

and sent to the Echigo front. My fourth brother, Shirō, was assigned to the Byakkotai, but was sick in bed with a chronic fever.

There were five females living in the house—my grandmother Tsune (eighty-four); my mother, Fuji (fifty); Taichirō's wife, Toku (twenty); and my sisters Soi (nineteen) and Satsu (seven). The domain had left the women's fates to the discretion of each family—whether they would leave Wakamatsu or help in the defense of the castle. I had no idea what my own family intended to do, or if some kind of agreement had been reached with relatives and friends.

I remember one of the first things my mother did was to drag my brother Shirō out of bed, help him put on his clothes and pair of swords, and order him to go straight to the castle. Sick and deathly pale, Shirō was barely able to walk. My mother took him by the hand and led him to the front gate, where the rest of the family had gathered to bid him farewell. My brother, though, stood motionless, looking bewildered. "Shirō!" my mother shouted. "Have you forgotten you are a son of the Shiba family? Your father is already at the castle. Go and join him at once, and do not bring shame on the family name." My grandmother also tried to rouse my brother's spirits: "I shall go one step ahead to the Land of the Dead and be waiting for you." At last, Shirō bowed to everyone and headed for the castle with unsteady steps. My mother wiped her tears with her kimono sleeves and disappeared into the house. Dazed, I remained standing at the gate until my grandmother persuaded me to go inside. For a while, I went about in a trance, at a complete loss for words.

The domain authorities issued an announcement: "In the event of a crisis, the fire bell will be sounded in rapid succession; women and children living in the samurai quarters are to hasten to the third enclosure of the castle." The women who decided to join in the defense of the castle had already taken up their posts; the rest were waiting at home in readiness.

The day after the announcement, one of the menservants came running down the hall to the room where the family usu-

ally gathered. "I have news, I have important news," he shouted. At this, my little sister, Satsu, who was sitting next to me, whipped out a dagger that she had tucked into her kimono and slipped off its case. My mother was appalled. She placed her hand on my sister's arm and said, "There's no need to be impetuous. When the time comes, the fire bell will give us adequate warning." The servant had come to tell us to be on the alert because enemy advance troops had been sighted near the city.

This was now the eighth month. On the morning of the twenty-first, my great-uncle Tsukane's widow, Kisa, who looked after our country home in Omokawasawa, came for a visit. She turned to me and said, "The mushrooms and chestnuts in the mountains are ripe for picking. Why don't you come and stay with me?" My mother immediately agreed. "Yes, you should go. School is closed, and all the men are at the castle anyway." She brought out my black Western-style clothes—the good suit I had not worn for some time—tucked a dagger into my belt, and gave me a hand towel, tissue, and other items that might be useful.* She then handed me a bamboo basket and urged me to hurry. The city was in turmoil, my friends no longer got together to play, my father and brothers were away and not expected to return for some time. For days, I had not heard the sound of laughter in our house. So, on a childish whim, on a rash impulse, I decided to go. I little dreamed that this would be a final leave-taking.

My grandmother, mother, and sisters came to the front gate to bid me good-bye. I bowed and set off with a light heart. Not for a moment did I suspect that they had seen me off knowing that we would not meet again in this world. The family had secretly decided that at least one son should live on to continue the family line and vindicate the honor of the domain. They had also decided not to have the women join in the defense of the castle; they would be useless in battle and needlessly consume

*For special occasions, samurai sons in Aizu seem to have worn Western clothes—a combination of trousers and a short, black wool jacket with fitted sleeves.

provisions. Instead, as soon as the enemy entered the city, the women would commit suicide rather than face dishonor. Even my seven-year-old sister had resolved to kill herself with her dagger. And I was too obtuse, too thickheaded, to have realized this. I was still young, it is true, but I shall never be able to forgive myself. Each time I think about it, I feel endless torment.

A Sea of Fire

I spent the night at the house in Omokawasawa, and the next day, accompanied by my great-aunt Kisa, I roamed the hills and marshes hunting for mushrooms and chestnuts. We returned to the house in the evening, and at my aunt's kind suggestion, I took a hot bath. Afterward, as I was playing outside with Tometarō, the son of the servant Tomekichi, a charcoal maker from Kuromori Village passed by on his way home from Waka-matsu. He told us that the city had been encircled by enemy troops and was in great confusion, but when I asked for further details, he said he did not know. Filled with foreboding, I wondered what I should do.

In a while, Tomekichi returned from Wakamatsu. "I have a message from your mother," he said. "The enemy is closing in and it's become quite dangerous. She wants you to come home tomorrow, right after sunrise. I am supposed to accompany you." I wanted to see my mother as soon as possible, and since I was unwilling to waste a minute, I demanded that we leave at once. Tomekichi would not consent, however, and insisted that we follow my mother's instructions. My great-aunt agreed, adding that it was too risky trying to find our way through enemy territory in the dark. I gave in, with much reluctance, and when I went to bed, sleep would not come. Sometime after midnight, it began to rain heavily.

The next morning, on the twenty-third, we left punctually

at six. I wore my black suit and dagger. In one hand, I carried
the basket of chestnuts and mushrooms I had picked, and in the
other, an umbrella Tomekichi had brought from my mother.
Tomekichi was dressed in his rainwear of straw cape and hat.
We made our way uphill on the muddy path for about five or
six hundred yards, but just as we reached Yamanokami, a vil-
lage across the [Sawa] river from Omokawasawa Honson, we
began hearing strange noises—a dull boom that crept along the
ground, then reverberated up into the mountains and shook the
air. I asked Tomekichi what it could be, but he claimed not to
know. We pressed on until we reached the pass at Nagarezaka.
Here we heard a steady *pop* that sounded like someone roast-
ing beans in a pan. That, together with the rain beating down
on my umbrella, made the noise deafening. Not until we passed
the villages of Negishi and Tsutsumisawa did it occur to me
that this was the sound of gunfire.

At the northern edge of Tsutsumisawa, we met straggling
groups of refugees, all soaked to the skin. Some held the elder-
ly by the arm, while others carried infants and invalids on their
back. Many women were armed with halberds and spears. Sev-
eral had as many as three or four swords. Everyone was bare-
foot, without straw rain capes or hats, let alone umbrellas. As
they emerged one after another from the mists of rain the line
of refugees seemed endless. Judging from their appearance, I
surmised that the city had been taken by surprise.

According to the chronicle *Furukawa Suetō jitsureki*, the fire
bell had been rung only after enemy advance troops had broken
through a gate in the outer wall and set fire to houses. Caught
off guard, the men who remained at home took up their swords
and raced to the third enclosure. Following them were the
women armed with halberds. But many arrived too late and
found the castle gates closed. The gathering crowd jostled for
space while exposed to enemy fire. At this moment—the chron-
icle continues—a man galloped by on horseback and shouted,
"Don't stay here—it's too dangerous. Go quickly to the south-
west, to the Kawaramachi Gate." The crowd followed these
instructions, but when they tried to go through the gate, they

were stopped by sentries, who insisted that the daimyo had ordered them to keep the gate closed. As the crowd stood helpless, the sixty-three-year-old Karasawa Chōkurō arrived at the scene. He berated the sentries, his hand gripping his sword as if he were about to slash them to pieces. After the crowd was finally allowed through the gate, they headed for the ferry crossing at the Ōkawa [Aga] River. Once there, they could not cross, for the river, swollen by the rain, was churning dangerously.

A peasant on the riverbank saw their plight and sounded the bell to call for help. Scores of peasants dressed in rainwear ran out of their houses. They commandeered the boats in the area and began ferrying the refugees. But progress was slow, since only a limited number of boats was available to transport thousands of people. Standing guard all day in the rain were the samurai women, who wore white headbands and held their halberds upright. The twelve- and thirteen-year-old Nisshinkan students also stood guard, each clutching a pair of swords. The peasants, no less courageous, rowed frantically back and forth against the raging currents, and though they were exhausted, they refused to rest. In the red glare of the approaching fire, they looked like the demon kings Ashura and Niō presiding over a scene in hell. The ear-splitting cannon fire and the heat from the flames intensified with each passing minute, but still the peasants would not abandon their task. The chronicle credits the peasants for the minimal loss of life.

The refugees we encountered near Tsutsumisawa had probably escaped in the same manner. They were fleeing south, while Tomekichi and I were heading north. Some of the people tried to stop me. "Where is your family, young master? And where are you going? As you see, the whole city's on fire—there's no way you can enter the castle precincts. Turn back before it's too late." "Young master, you can't go home now. Turn back, I'm telling you, turn back."

I looked in the direction of Wakamatsu. Black clouds billowed up into the sky, smoke shrouded the donjon and turrets of the castle, and tongues of flame shot up all over the city. But I was desperate to reach my mother. I ignored their advice and

paid no heed to the gunfire. I tore myself away from the crowd and ran splashing across the rice fields that bordered the road. Tomekichi reluctantly followed.

I reached the northern edge of Kitaoyama Village, where the road forked to Nakano. I looked for the castle again. This time, I dimly made out the white walls of the donjon and turrets through the thick smoke. The area near my house, however, was submerged in waves of fire.

Tomekichi caught up with me and then stopped in his tracks. He said that he did not see how we could enter the city. I had to agree, and in despair, I threw my arms around a stone road marker and fell to my knees. I cried out "Mother, Mother" over and over, pummeled the ground, tore at the grass, and wept aloud. At length, Tomekichi pulled me to my feet. "Young master, I know how you feel, but there is nothing we can do. We could try going in through the Minamimachi Gate perhaps . . ." Heartened by his words, I headed for Nakano Village, but even from a distance, I could see that it was impossible to enter the city.

Tomekichi tried to console me. "Young master, let's go back to the house at Omokawasawa. Your mother and the rest of the family are sure to be there. Why, they may even be among those refugees. Let's hurry." He said he would first get some information from a friend in the village and instructed me to go ahead. I had no choice. Though it was still raining heavily, I folded my umbrella, tucked it under my arm, and fell in behind the line of refugees. In this manner, I retraced the five miles back to Omokawasawa.

The people around me panted with each step, too tired to talk. Even the children, pulled along by their elders, stumbled on in stolid silence, their faces streaked with mud. The refugees were alive, but to me they looked more like a band of wraiths.

A Night of Despair

In Omokawasawa, I found the house overrun by refugees. Complete strangers—at least a hundred—filled the rooms, huddled under the eaves, or stood in the garden drenched by the rain. Several had even cajoled my great-aunt Kisa and Tomekichi's wife to cook rice for them and acted as if they owned the place. Among the crowd I recognized Ina Hanroku, a samurai of distinguished lineage, who had come with his retainers, but I could not find my mother or other members of the family anywhere.

My aunt and Tomekichi's wife ran to me as soon as they saw me. They asked for news of the family, but of course I could tell them nothing. Several refugees noticed us talking and realized that I was the young master of the house. They bowed deferentially and tried to cheer me up: "Oh, your family is bound to come soon." Clinging to a glimmer of hope, I stood by the entrance and searched the gathering crowd for a familiar face. Though it was almost midday, I had no desire to eat.

At about two, my maternal aunt Hinata Hide arrived with her five children—Oyoshi, Orin, Shinsaburō, Shinshirō, and Shingorō. But my aunt, too, did not know of the family's whereabouts. Presently, my great-uncle Shiba Seisuke (seventy years old), who lived in Omokawa Village, came with his wife, Tada. They looked utterly exhausted. I asked for news of the

family, but my uncle merely answered in a low voice, "Wait till later," and went into the house.

My uncle cleared the inner room of the refugees and beckoned me to come and sit in front of him. Drawing himself up straight, he began to speak. "It happened this morning. The enemy was already in the city, but your mother and the rest of the women in the family refused to leave the house. They committed suicide—yes, all five—your mother, your grandmother, your sisters Soi and Satsu, and Taichirō's wife, Toku. I administered the final blow at their request.* I then set fire to the house and came here. As her last wish, your mother asked me to take care of you.

"I realize that this is very painful for you, but you and I both know that this is the lot of samurai. You must not become distraught or give in to unseemly grief. You are to resign yourself and accept your fate with grace and fortitude. I want you to know that your own little sister killed herself with great courage and determination. From this day forward, you are to bear up and do as I say."

I looked at my uncle blankly, too stunned to speak, even to cry. Suddenly, my head began to swim, and I fainted away. I have no idea how long I remained unconscious, but in the middle of the night, I was awakened by someone tapping me on the shoulder. It was my uncle Seisuke. He lit the oil lamp and told me to sit up.

"Enemy troops have burned down the city and laid siege to the castle. They are certain to look for samurai outside the castle precincts. They're the kind of scoundrels who think nothing of killing the womenfolk of townsmen and peasants. They even leave the corpses of women strewn along the streets, though the peasant men have been covering them with straw mats as they flee. You never know what those good-for-nothing potato samurai will do next. The way you look now, anyone can tell

*When a person commits ritual suicide, the final blow is administered by decapitation.

right away you're from a samurai family. And since your mother asked me to take care of you, I've decided to have you dress like a peasant boy for your own safety."

Although I remained silent, my uncle motioned to my aunt Kisa to come in and help him cut off my topknot. They cropped my hair close to the skull, dressed me in an old kimono and pair of leggings that belonged to Tomekichi's son. They stowed my Western suit and pair of swords in the loft. "This should do. But do not go outside without my permission." With these words, my uncle left the room. I lay down on the quilts and fell asleep to the sound of rain. It was to be the last day in my life as a samurai son.

The days passed, and one by one, the refugees drifted away. My aunt Hide's family and ten or so acquaintances stayed on. In a while, my aunt's family left, too, but unable to find anyone willing to take them in, they soon returned.

Uncle Seisuke's grandson Arakawa Toranosuke and I were the same age. Tomekichi's son Tometarō was a couple of years younger, and my cousins Hinata Shinsaburō and Shinshirō were a year older and a year younger. They made perfect playmates. I played with them during the day, and the distraction momentarily eased the pain, but at night, for a full two months, I dreamed about my mother and sisters—about the family sitting happily together—and woke up each time with a start.

It was the middle of the ninth month. The sound of shelling from Wakamatsu had not ceased. In fact, one day, Satsuma soldiers had come all the way to Omokawasawa in pursuit of Naitō Kain, a domain elder, who had taken shelter with his family at the Taiunji Temple. Surrounded, he and his family committed suicide.

Then, unexpectedly, on the twentieth, my brother Taichirō arrived, carried on a stretcher by Jinmori Heizō and several subordinates. Under orders from castle headquarters, he had been fighting near Ichinoseki but had been shot in the leg. I had long since given him up for dead, and I was so happy to see him that I ran around the house announcing the news. My uncle and everyone in the Hinata family rushed out to greet my

brother and took him inside to tend to his wound. Unable to stand, he barely managed to crawl across the tatami mat with his hands and one leg. The same day, my uncle told him what had happened to the family; I knew only too well the sorrow and pain my brother must have felt.

My brother worried that he would be captured if he stayed on in the house. So after dismissing his other men, he asked Heizō and me to carry him to a ravine eight hundred yards deep in the mountains. The ravine was rather ominously called Dead Man's Gorge, but it was secluded and well hidden. We chose a spot near a spring, laid down a bed of boards about the size of two tatami mats, covered it with rough straw mats, and put a thick layer of green branches overhead. Here the three of us would stay, safe from enemy eyes.

Heizō's job was to nurse Taichirō's wound. Each day, he drew springwater into a water pistol he had fashioned from a length of bamboo, squirted the wound, and covered it with a piece of white cotton. I easily passed for a peasant boy, so my job was to wait until dark, when no one was around. Then I would fetch food from the house and bury the soiled bandages in the ground.

One day, we received a warning that enemy troops were in the vicinity. The Hinata family came to join us, and we helped Taichirō along as we all went farther into the mountains. Taking shelter under our umbrellas, we pitched camp in a grove of pine trees.

Meanwhile, the sound of gunfire from Wakamatsu continued without even a moment's pause. We felt much anxiety as we speculated about the outcome. My aunt Kisa and Uncle Seisuke's wife, Tada, were of the opinion that when the shooting stopped, it meant all was lost—that the daimyo and everyone else in the castle had died. But Heizō, who was young and hotheaded, would have none of this, and whenever he heard of enemy troops approaching, he would run out with his gun and sword, only to be restrained by my brother.

Heizō came from the village of Nigorigawa in Echigo Province. He was fond of sumo and had been the champion

wrestler in his village. He was also fond of gambling and regularly got into fights. But at the same time, he was a man of strong loyalties and considered himself a friend of the weak and downtrodden. In the fifth month, he had been hired as a servant by my uncle Shiba Morizō (later Kōzuki Sagonosuke), who was fighting on the Echigo front. Heizō came to relish the experience of war and eagerly fought at the front line of battle. My uncle sustained a wound, however, and Heizō had to nurse him. As soon as my uncle recovered, Heizō returned to Echigo to fight, this time under the command of my brother, the region's military commissioner.

The Aizu forces had to retreat, and on the morning of the twenty-third of the eighth month, my brother and his men reached Tabanematsu, on the outskirts of Wakamatsu. They looked in the direction of the castle, but saw only fire and smoke. My brother pointed at the scene and said, "Wakamatsu has fallen into enemy hands. Our only course is to join the men in the castle and fight to the death. But you, Heizō, have no ties whatsoever with Aizu and are under no obligation to die with us. Go home, quickly." Handing some money to Heizō, he bid him farewell.

Heizō was furious. "This comes as a terrible shock, sir. I cannot believe that my own master would say anything so pitiless and unkind. I may be a lowly gambler, but I am not the sort to forget a favor, whether it is a night's lodging or bowl of rice. At a time when my master's domain is in grave danger, I consider it my duty to offer up my life in its defense. Yet I now hear that I am to leave because my master is returning to the castle in its hour of need. This would be an act of sheer ingratitude and heartlessness. These may be your orders, sir, but I must refuse." With this, Heizō sat himself down on the ground, red with indignation and determined not to budge an inch. My brother relented. They did not go to the castle, but instead the two fought on various fronts until my brother was wounded at Ichinoseki on the nineteenth day of the ninth month.

I am jumping ahead with my story, but after the end of the hostilities, Taichirō was taken to a hospital. Assured that his

master was in good hands, Heizō asked for permission to leave Taichirō's service. He would once again become a gambler and roam about as he wished. Wearing one sword, he then took off without further ado.

After that there was no news from Heizō, but five years later, in Meiji 6 [1873], when I was a student at the Army Cadet School, I unexpectedly received a letter from him. The envelope was addressed to Shiba Gorō, Institute of Learning, Former Residence of the Honorable Ii Kamon-no-kami [Naosuke]. He asked about the family, and I immediately wrote back. Instead of answering, Heizō himself came to see me. I took him to see my brother, who was staying temporarily at the Sensōji Temple in Asakusa. Our reunion made us shed tears of joy at having come through the years unharmed. Heizō said he had settled down, found a place to live opposite the Kichijōji Temple in Komagome, taken a wife, and opened a rice-husking shop.

Heizō came to visit from time to time, and in the autumn following our reunion, he invited my brother and me to dine with him at the home of a farmer living near Dangozaka in Komagome. It was the height of the chrysanthemum season. The meal was simple but served in a most hospitable manner. After we had finished eating, Heizō bowed low and pressed his hands together on the tatami. "As you know, I decided to mend my ways and make an honest living. I have somehow managed until now, but I am really not cut out for it. I don't think I can last much longer. You see, a gambler's only happy when he's with his cronies. And besides, it doesn't look as though there'll be another war. I really have nothing to look forward to. I have made up my mind to pull up stakes and wander about again, and that is why I asked you here today. I cannot tell you how very honored I am to have you here this evening."

Taichirō tried to dissuade him, but some time later, when I went by his house, I saw no trace of the shop. Heizō was thirty-six at the time of the Boshin War, so he must have been forty-one or forty-two when we met that evening. He was a good man, and I very much regret not seeing him again.

Last Days
of the Bakufu

As I remember, it happened on the twenty-second day of the
ninth month. I was at the house in Omokawasawa when the
shooting suddenly stopped. Taichirō had partially recovered by
then and was hobbling about with the aid of a cane. The sud-
den stillness, coming after a month of constant gunfire, made us
even more uneasy and left us with an eerie sense of emptiness.
The cloudless, late-autumn sky, a vault of brilliant blue, seemed
incongruous and strange, and the thin wavering line of red
dragonflies, survivors of the autumn season, only added to the
feeling of despair that gripped us.

Full of trepidation, the villagers came out of hiding to see
what had happened to the city. Rumors flew: "The daimyo and
all the men in the castle fought to the bitter end." Or, "When
the castle was taken, everyone committed *seppuku*," or again,
"They've surrendered, and the daimyo, his son, and almost
everyone else is unharmed and well." Anxious to know the
truth, I studied my uncle and brother's faces for some clue, but
they went about impassively, lost in thought. My aunts Kisa
and Tada were silent, too, and refrained from talking even to
one another. My young companions no longer asked me to join
them, nor did I make any overtures. Left on my own, I walked
up a mountain path for a glimpse of the city. Peering through
the scarlet-tinged leaves, I could not help thinking that my

mother was still there, just beyond the silver white waves of
pampas grass. I wept inconsolably.

Our servant Tomekichi, who had been sent to Wakamatsu
to reconnoiter, soon returned to tell us that the castle had
indeed surrendered and been delivered to the enemy. Although
we had prepared ourselves for the worst, we were nevertheless
shaken and fell into a deep silence.

My uncle Seisuke, until then strong-willed and stoical,
finally broke down and wept. Taichirō covered his eyes with
clenched fists, and my aunts collapsed into tears. All of a sud-
den, Heizō gave a howl of rage and leapt down into the garden.
He seized Tomekichi by the collar and knocked him down to
the ground. "What are you saying? We would never surrender!
I may be a mere servant, but I know the way of the warrior.
How dare you sully your daimyo's name!" But even as he
lashed out, he was crying. Falling to his knees, he faced the fam-
ily and began to bow. In doing so, he hit his head over and over
against the ground.

Trembling, Tomekichi continued. "It grieves me terribly,
but the castle really has surrendered. The daimyo and his
family are safe and have moved to the Myōkokuji Temple
outside the castle precincts. A great many of the men were
wounded, but I heard that morale is high and that no one has
committed any shameful acts. All the men were allowed to
leave the castle wearing their swords and have been sent
under guard to Inawashiro. Enemy troops swarmed the road-
side and shouted abuses, spat on them, and hurled rocks, but
our men remained calm and never lost control of themselves.
The approximately 570 women in the castle have been sent
to Hamasaki, near Kitakata, along with the men who surren-
dered outside the castle. I regret to say that I was unable to
obtain information about your father and brothers, but I am
quite sure they are safe." Too agitated to go on, Tomekichi
began to sob.

Taichirō tried to comfort him, holding back his own tears.
"Thank you—you've done a splendid job of gathering all this

information. I now believe that the castle truly has fallen. But what of the rest of the city? Did you hear anything?"

"Nothing certain, sir. The castle precincts have been reduced to ashes. There isn't a thing left. Most of the houses in the city have burned down, too. Those remaining have been confiscated by enemy soldiers and marked with signs. The commoner women who were captured have been sent to work as servants. There's been talk of violence and heinous deeds, but it's hard to know just what is happening. I have heard that the samurai women in Hamasaki are being treated with courtesy and have been given clothes to protect themselves against the cold. The enemy may be the worst kind of samurai, but they're samurai all the same and have shown some compassion."

My brother thanked Tomekichi and dismissed him. He then turned to Heizō, who remained prostrate on the ground. "Heizō, I am as saddened and angered as you are, but for now we must make every effort not to behave like fools. It is the least that's expected of samurai. Until we receive further orders, we must try not to act rashly." My brother tried to reason with him, but Heizō refused to get up. My aunt Kisa could not bear to look on any longer. She stepped down into the garden and gently persuaded him to go with her to the back of the house.

And thus it was that Aizu, the last bastion of the Tokugawa *bakufu*, finally met its end.

A Time of Trial
for the Family

During the previous few decades, the *bakufu* had been beset by troubles from within and without and had repeatedly turned to Aizu for help. [As early as 1807], when Russian troops landed on the islands of Rebun and Rishiri off the northern tip of Ezo [Hokkaido], the *bakufu* had determined that the Matsùmae domain was inadequate to the task and had ordered Aizu to send troops to repel the foreigners. The Aizu samurai built fortifications in Wakkanai, Notsukeushi, and other sites and succeeded in ejecting the Russians, but subsequently, many of these samurai had fallen victim to sickness and died. All that remained on the bleak northern coast was a scattering of graves and stones marking the site of the encampments. Then, more recently [in 1862], the *bakufu* had appointed the Aizu daimyo Katamori as Kyoto protector to keep the peace in the imperial capital. With responsibilities in both Kyoto and Edo, Aizu men had literally "run back and forth from east to west."

[Earlier, in 1856], the year after the Great Ansei Earthquake had leveled most of Edo, the American diplomat Townsend Harris had arrived, demanding the establishment of a consular office [in accordance with a friendship treaty signed in 1854]. The *bakufu* reluctantly complied, but the extremist *rōnin*, who opposed the opening of the country, called for the expulsion of the "barbarians" and resorted to terrorist acts. *Rōnin* from Satsuma and Chōshū were particularly active. In the face of

continued violence, British warships fired on Kagoshima [1863], and soon after, the combined fleet of Britain, France, the United States, and Holland bombarded Shimonoseki [1864]. Having thus experienced firsthand the military might of the "barbarians," Satsuma and Chōshū quickly reversed their positions and put all their energies into bringing down the *bakufu*. In truth, the past few years had been a time of great turbulence.

As a child I had been unaware of the complexities of politics. But now, with the country awakened from three centuries of slumber, I would come to know the harsh realities of the world. To be sure, for a man, it was worthwhile to be alive at such a time and to be witness to the renewal of a nation. But what of my grandmother, my mother, and my sisters, who had paid so dearly with their lives? How could I ever make it up to them? And what of the innocent peasants and townspeople in Wakamatsu who saw their possessions looted, families slaughtered, and women raped? The memory was too cruel to contemplate.

At the end of the tenth month, people other than samurai were given permission to enter the city. My brother ordered Tomekichi to go to our house on Hon Ninochō and gather the charred remains of the family. Afraid of being caught, Tomekichi stole into the grounds under cover of night, and after roughly determining the place where they had died, searched through the ashes with his bare hands. He collected only the larger bones, but with no time to take them to Erinji, our family temple, he hid in a corner of the Kōtokuji Temple near the outer wall's Babaguchi Gate. He then buried the bones in a stranger's grave, marked the spot with a piece of wood, and hurried back.

The next month, I went to the house with my aunts Kisa and Tada. To all appearances a peasant boy, I was presumably safe. At the house, we found nothing but a mound of tiles and stones, all scorched a rust red. The force of the fire must have been terrible, for most of the trees in the garden had burned down. I stood amid the ruins and looked around in a daze.

Every last house in the samurai quarters had been razed; not an object remained to obstruct my view. I looked up toward the castle. Scarred by cannon fire, its white walls blistered and roof tiles broken loose, the castle reminded me of a wounded warrior struggling to get to his feet. It was piteous to behold, an utterly heartbreaking sight. I was struck anew by the bitter fact of defeat and collapsed, dry-eyed, onto the pile of rubble.

"Gorō-sama," my aunts said. "We know it's very hard for you, but do get up. Look, we're women but we're standing up straight, aren't we? You really must get up. The spirits of your grandmother and mother and sisters are wandering near us. You don't want them to see you like this. Gorō-sama, we beg you to get up." Supported by my aunts, I managed to get to my feet, but then they began to weep.

The area was deserted—not an enemy soldier could be seen, there was not a soul gathering bones. The leaden winter sky hung low, as if to cast a pall over the tragic scene. My aunts handed me a pair of chopsticks. "Here, Gorō-sama, use these to collect the bones of your dear ones. And put them in this paper bag." I sifted through the ashes, but as I picked up the tiny fragments, I thought to myself: Is this what has become of my grandmother, mother, and sisters? Though their fate was beyond imagining, the tears flowed unchecked down my cheeks. I scrambled about in the rubble, desperate to find a living object, and came upon the stump of a camellia bush that had once stood in a corner of the garden. This I dug up and took back to Omokawasawa. The bush took root, and from what I heard, eventually grew to full height.

On our way back, we stopped at the burnt remains of the house of a relative, Nakazawa Jūrō. We searched for the bones of the family, but finding none, assumed that someone had already come to collect them.[3]

Sometime later, we recovered the bones that Tomekichi had hidden at Kōtokuji. We asked my sister Tsuma to come from Kitakata, where she was living with her in-laws, the Mochizuki family, and put all the bones, including those I had collected, in a white cedar box. We placed this box on the family altar. We

subsequently had the bones formally interred in the family grave at Erinji. We asked Nagasaka-sensei, an acquaintance in Keizan Village, to write an epitaph describing the tragic deaths of my grandmother, mother, and sisters. (The tombstone was rebuilt later.)

We were to stay in Omokawasawa for nine months, passing the days in idleness, since we did not have anything to do. Winter set in, and as each day brought fresh snow, the fields and mountains turned a gleaming white. One particularly cold morning, when the chill seemed to pierce our bones, my brother Shirō appeared unannounced. Seeing him standing in the snow, Taichirō and I, along with everyone in the house, thought we were dreaming and dared not speak lest he vanish like a phantom. The lone figure took off his sedge hat, brushed the snow from his clothes, and bowed, smiling faintly. It was Shirō, beyond a doubt.

With a cry of surprise, my aunts ran outside and made a big fuss over him. Then they brought him into the house. My uncle Seisuke, who was too shocked to get up, dissolved into tears. He had become querulous of late—not at all like his former self—and taken to bewailing the fickleness of this world night and day. The samurai spirit was dead, he said, and the Shinto gods, even the Buddha, were not to be trusted. Other times, he would criticize the northeastern domains for their cowardice in deserting Aizu or fulminate against the excesses of the samurai from Satsuma, Chōshū, Tosa, and Higo. And in the end, he would heave a sigh and say, What's the use, everything is over and done with. Even now, with Shirō safely back, he seemed incapable of a spirited reaction and just kept repeating in a quavering voice, "You're alive, oh, thank goodness, thank goodness, you're alive . . ."

As I mentioned earlier, Shirō was in bed with a fever at the time of the attack but had been forced by my mother to go to the castle. He was assigned to the Byakkotai, but because he was still sick he had reluctantly taken to bed in the castle. He had survived while most of the young men in his unit had perished.

Taichirō blinked back his tears and asked Shirō for news of

the family. My father had apparently been slightly wounded but was now fully recovered; my third brother, Gosaburō, was unharmed. All three were at the detention camp in Inawashiro, but Shirō had been given special permission to visit us for one day only. He said he was greatly relieved to find us safe and well.

It had been several months since we last saw each other. There was much news to share, but whenever the talk turned to our grandmother, mother, and sisters, we would be overcome by sorrow and anger and unable to go on. Both Shirō and I had left home at our mother's bidding and as a result, we were alive. By the cruelest twist of fate, only the men in the family had survived.

Taichirō persuaded my uncle to go to bed. We three sat by the hearth and talked far into the night. According to Shirō, the women in the castle had played an extremely courageous part in the defense. Whenever a cannonball landed, they ran to the spot and covered it with wet mats and rice sacks before it could explode. They cooked meals and nursed the wounded without respite, heedless of the damage to their clothes. Bespattered with blood, they had outdone themselves in helping the men. And they had been fully prepared, if necessary, to change into their white kimono and charge into the enemy with their halberds.[4]

Outside, the wind blustered and roared. The snow continued to drift down. Once in a while the snow would slide down the eaves, and fanned by the gusts of air rushing through the crevices, the flames in the hearth would flicker back and forth. As I talked to my brothers, I remembered how I had sat on my mother's lap. I could almost feel her gentle touch as she dressed me in the morning, and I furtively wiped my tears. Had it not been for my elderly grandmother and young sisters, my mother would have surely joined the women in the castle and acquitted herself gloriously. As I thought about her in this way, I missed her even more.

Shirō departed the next morning. As he was about to go, he noticed my thin clothes and gave me the white padded vest my mother had made him wear the day he left for the castle.

Little by little, we established contact with our other relatives. We learned that my sister Kayo, and her husband Kimura

Hyōgo, who had been wounded and immobilized, as well as everyone else in their family had committed suicide. Nine in all. A young retainer, Yakichi, and their maid Sei set fire to the house before escaping, and later, braving enemy fire, they returned to collect the bones. They buried the bones temporarily at the Hokkeji Temple. My aunt's family, the Nakazawas, also died in the same manner, as did my cousin Suwa Takenosuke's wife. My paternal uncle Shiba Morizō had been sent to Sendai on a mission, but was presently with [Enomoto Takeaki and] the remnants of the *bakufu* forces in Hakodate. My maternal uncle Hinata Saemon and his oldest son, Shintarō, were killed in battle. My sister Tsuma, who married into the Mochizuki family, was at the detention camp in Kitakata with her children and in-laws. She came to see us now and then, and we went together to visit the family grave at Erinji. The roads were buried in snow, and returning home in the dark was not easy.

Tsuma sometimes brought her children. She held her older daughter, Oman, by the hand, had her son Ryūtarō strapped to her back, and her youngest, Osen, was tucked inside her kimono front. She would stop midway for a short rest at the Hinata's temporary home in Oyama, go through five more miles of snow-covered roads, and arrive late at night. She was twenty-six at the time. Life was harsh for one so young, and I think of her now with great affection.

A hospital was set up in Oyama with facilities open to friend and foe alike. Taichirō was taken on Tomekichi's pack-horse to have his leg treated. On the way home, he stayed at the Ashinomaki Hot Springs for four or five days. I was allowed to join him and can still recall the pleasurable sensation of soaking in the hot water.

I spent most of the time in my brother's company, but with no books, brushes, or ink at hand, I was unable to take lessons from him. More often than not, I wandered off to visit the Hinata family in Oyama or my uncle Seisuke, who had left our house a while earlier. I usually stayed the longest at my uncle's house, where I could play with Yamaguchi Toranoshin and Numasawa Einosuke. Occasionally, at my aunt Tada's request,

I would go to the mountains with Toranoshin to gather chestnuts, persimmons, and other wild fruit. We would sit on a mat in front of a roadside memorial stone called the Yudonoyama Kuyōtō and offer these items for sale. I also went to Toranoshin's house to help him load the rice sheaves onto an ox for transport to market. I was now a peasant boy in all respects, and my uncle, who recognized this, made no effort to stop me. He even seemed to encourage me in these activities, and for my part, I was quite content to go about with hair shorn and leggings caked with mud.

Shirō came to visit my uncle one day and was shocked to see what I was doing. He angrily confronted my uncle, digging his right fist into the tatami and demanding, "Dear uncle, would you kindly tell me what is happening? Gorō may be dressed like a peasant, but he is, may I remind you, a son of the Shiba family. Though he's discarded his sword and cut off his hair, he is still the son of a samurai. Would you please tell me what you have in mind."

My uncle muttered something inaudible. Shirō continued to upbraid him. "It is my understanding that Mother's dying wish was for you to look after Gorō. I cannot think that she meant for you to make him a peasant. We may have lost the war, but we should not behave in a demeaning manner. You yourself should be aware of this. There's no need to go out of one's way to degrade oneself. What am I to say when I report back to my father?" But my uncle had long since lost the will to crawl out of the depths of despair. The same day, Shirō stopped by the house in Omokawasawa to talk privately with Taichirō about my future.

Spring came. It was the second year of Meiji [1869]. The snow melted at last, and once again, wild cherry blossoms colored the mountains. Summer followed quickly, and as if to rise above the joys and sorrows of the mortal world, soft breezes rippled through the fresh green leaves. Delighted with the warm weather and oblivious to my brother's worries, I passed the hours mingling happily with the peasants. But there was one change: Taichirō acquired a brush and ink and started giving me calligraphy lessons.

Detention Camp in Edo

Most of the wounded at the Oyama Hospital had completed their course of treatment, and in the sixth month, the Aizu men were ordered to go under guard to Edo as prisoners of war.

The people in Aizu were outraged. From the outset, Aizu had never intended to put up armed resistance. The shogun had surrendered his governing authority, Katamori had resigned from his post as Kyoto protector, and to avoid war, he had returned to Wakamatsu to live in seclusion. The government had nevertheless branded Aizu a rebel domain, an enemy of the court, and sent a punitive army. The invading troops, furthermore, had inflicted unspeakable acts of violence on the populace and subjected them to untold misery. The castle was in ruins, and apart from samurai swords, all weapons had been confiscated. What more did they want?

I spoke to Taichirō. "If Satsuma and Chōshū intend to flaunt their might by taking us to Edo as prisoners and parade us through the streets like common criminals, I wish to stay in Aizu. I will become a peasant and watch over Mother's grave." My brother reacted angrily. "Listen, we've got to see this to the end and find out what the rascals from Satsuma and Chōshū are up to. If they intend to humiliate us, we'll fight to the death—in Edo or anywhere. Or else we'll slash open our bellies and show them what Aizu men are made of. If you lose your nerve now, what are you going to do in the future? Everything,

do you hear, *everything* begins at this moment!" I hung my head and nodded.

It seemed unlikely that we would ever return to Aizu, so Taichirō gave Tomekichi the fields and forest we owned in Omokawasawa in recognition of many years of faithful service.⁵ He also left the villagers a grove of cedars to repair the houses that had been damaged in the fighting. The trees were felled at a later date.

On the eve of his departure for Edo, Taichirō decided to take me along. The wounded prisoners had been told that, depending on rank, they would be allowed to take along a personal attendant. Aware that a member of his own family, even a child, would not be permitted to accompany him, he submitted a request to take a family servant, Kanome Tomekichi. Permission was granted. The government troops must have known who this eleven-year-old attendant was, but chose to overlook it.

The rainy season had begun. It drizzled and poured day after day, without a gleam of sunlight. We tramped on the muddy road, but Taichirō was unable to walk with his bad leg and was given permission to use a litter. This litter was a simple contraption made of a wooden board with two poles. On this he sat, shielded from the rain by a sedge hat and straw mat, while I followed behind, wearing my hat and straw mat.

On the first day, we marched from Oyama to Takisawa, but the next day, weighed down by my rain-soaked straw mat, I was barely able to move. A guard took pity on me and requisitioned a litter. I climbed on, wrapped the old mat around my shoulders, and continued the journey swaying to and fro in the rain.

Thinking back on it, we must have looked like a procession of beggars: men with arms in slings, others limping on crutches, still others struggling to keep up but gradually falling behind, and not least of all, the gray-haired elderly carried piggyback by their attendants. We walked in complete silence, each burdened with his own fate. We had not the faintest inkling of what lay ahead and would slog on as long as our strength held out.

There were a little more than a hundred prisoners in our group, and this included former *bakufu* troops [who had fought in the area]. For some reason we had been grouped into units of five or six and told to leave space between us as we walked. I belonged to Unit Three, which was made up of Riki-nosuke, who was the oldest son of Elder Yanase Sanzaemon, Uchida Chūnoshin, a man named Itō, another named Kōsaka, and a former *bakufu* infantry officer who was acting as proxy for the elderly Higuchi Hayanoshin.*

We covered twelve to fourteen miles daily—a pace neither too fast nor too slow. Although it was my first trip to Edo, I felt no sense of anticipation, nor did I see anything to arouse my curiosity. The peasants and townspeople along the road seemed indifferent, as if they had become accustomed to war.[6] Once in a while, we would encounter samurai from other domains, but they, too, merely acknowledged us with a nod and showed no interest. This, I assume, was a part of samurai etiquette.

The grueling march took more than ten days. If I remember correctly, we reached Edo early in the seventh month, just at the end of the rainy season. The heat was oppressive, and we were utterly exhausted and dripping with sweat as we staggered into the Otsukiya, the former *bakufu* storehouse just inside the Hitotsubashi Gate [to Edo Castle]. The men who arrived ahead of us had already settled in and welcomed us newcomers.

The storehouse was a large, two-storied wooden structure with an earthen ground floor. We suspected it had been used to store pickles, for an odor of pickled radish still remained in the damp and stifling building. The storehouse now went by the name of Kinshinsho—the Place of Disciplinary Confinement.

Rows of coarse tatami mats had been set down on each side of a center aisle. There was one tatami mat for each person. From one end of the aisle, you could see the entire sixty-foot length of the long room. To mark the occasion of our arrival, our evening meal consisted of a piece of dried fish, a big bowl

*The elderly samurai who were too feeble to go to Edo seem to have been permitted to send proxies instead.

of rice, and miso soup ladled from a huge bucket. At night, however, we were unable to sleep. Not only was the building poorly ventilated, but it was infested with flies and mosquitoes. These were unsanitary conditions, to say the least. In desperation, many of the men got up in the middle of the night and removed some of the wooden wallboards. The next day, Taichirō found a tattered mosquito net somewhere, and we were able to sleep undisturbed.

The Aizu samurai who were sent to Edo were quartered in four camps: the Gokokuji Temple in Otowa; the Kōbusho (that is, the former *bakufu* Military Academy in Ogawamachi—later called Misaki-chō); the Kōda residence in Azabu (later the site of the Konoe Third Regiment); and our camp, the Otsukiya. A fifth camp was later established at the Zōjōji Temple in Shiba. All five were known as the Place of Disciplinary Confinement, but were actually prisoner of war camps and kept under guard.

Being kept under guard did not mean that our movements were restricted at all times. We would make up some excuse about how we needed medicine and so could always take turns getting a permit to leave camp. The men who had come as proxies were also free to go out. And if anyone slipped out and failed to return, there was no attempt to track him down. But then, as one might expect, the Aizu men had their pride as samurai and rarely went off without a good reason. The family was scattered—my father, at the Kōbusho; Gosaburō, at the Kōda residence; and Shirō, at Gokokuji. Still, we were able to see each other.

In time, the domain was given permission to set up a central liaison office at the former fire brigade office in Iida-chō. The former elder Yamakawa Ōkura was appointed head administrator, and he assembled a staff of domain officials and several influential men. He was put in charge of communication and coordination between the various camps. Such was the ostensible purpose, but in fact, he and his staff hoped to use the office to negotiate favorable terms for the domain.

Taichirō was assigned to the new office. He changed his name to Matsushima Suian and let his hair grow long so that

he looked like a doctor. As a samurai, he would be restricted to domain affairs, but as a doctor, he hoped to visit his friends and acquaintances from other domains, that is, the people he had met while working in Kyoto and Edo.* Then, when the time came for the government to determine Aizu's future, he would be able to turn to these people for support. He also gathered around him the brighter and more promising youths from Aizu and began giving a series of lectures. The group included Shirō and [my nephew] Kimura Ushitoku. It was my distinct impression that the formal lectures, long in abeyance, did much to reawaken the young men's self-awareness as samurai sons.

For some time, the new government had been moving ahead with plans to send settlers to Hokkaido to open up the territory. Aizu men were also encouraged to go, with the understanding that they would be set free and be allowed to have their families in the detention centers in Aizu and Niigata [Takata] join them. The response was surprisingly strong, and by the end, two hundred families applied.

With Taichirō away at the liaison office, I was on my own at the camp. In the eighth month, however, I was given permission to join him. Unlike the camp, the meals at the office were served in proper dishes on individual trays, as they were in samurai households. It had been almost a year since I had eaten in this manner. Moved by memories of home, I hesitated before picking up my chopsticks.

On the twenty-seventh day of the ninth month, the government informed the Aizu daimyo that he had been graciously granted 30,000 *koku* of land in the Nanbu domain as a place to conduct proper rites for domain ancestors. The government had previously asked the domain whether it wished to be relocated in Inawashiro or in Mutsu Province. Many had objected to the first choice because a small portion of former domain land was deemed both economically and psychologically unfeasible. The second choice, Mutsu, was admittedly unknown ter-

*Taichirō worked for several years at the Kuyōgata, the office that handled external affairs for the Kyoto protector.

ritory but much larger, and the Aizu men had decided to entrust their future to the land in the extreme north.

The domain was next notified that Tokugawa Yoshinobu, Katamori, and others [who had been on the *bakufu* side] had been pardoned by imperial decree. Katamori took this occasion to relinquish the family headship to his one-year-old son, Keisaburō, and the child, renamed Matsudaira Kataharu, became the new head of the daimyo house. Shortly thereafter, on the fourth day of the eleventh month, Kataharu was made a member of the new nobility.* Overjoyed by the turn of events, the Aizu men shed tears of gratitude and praised His Majesty for his unchanging grace and benevolence.

But I was completely baffled. What did they mean by pardoning us for our crimes? The villains from Satsuma and Chōshū were the ones to blame. What was all this talk about Aizu being wrong and being forgiven? I was angered by the injustice of it all, but when I saw the hopeful faces of my elders, who were congratulating each other on the restoration of the daimyo house, I could not bring myself to question them. Much later, I was to learn that the *bakufu* itself had repeatedly abolished domains for such offenses as internal dissension. So I suppose there was cause to celebrate now that Aizu had been spared extinction and was allowed to continue as a domain, at least in name.

The Aizu domain had originally been assessed at 300,000 *koku*. To this, 50,000 had been added over the years, and with Katamori's appointment as Kyoto protector, the domain had received a first emolument of 50,000 *koku*, and a second one of 55,000. To defray the costs of maintaining a force in Kyoto, it had also received a monthly allotment of two thousand bales of rice and ten thousand *ryō* in gold coins. In terms of rice income, Aizu had been a huge domain of 679,000 *koku* at one time. But Aizu was now a paltry 30,000 *koku*—a tract of volcanic terrain that had been confiscated from the Nanbu domain in Mutsu Province. This was humiliating in the extreme, yet the Aizu men

*All daimyo were made members of the new nobility (*kazoku*).

were shedding tears of gratitude, putting all their hopes into this most barren of lands. They had no idea that their new domain was snowbound half the year and that its actual yield was closer to 7,000 *koku*. The land would never support the samurai families, but who was to know?

The domain was soon given two new residential compounds, one at the Sōma residence inside the Shinbashi Gate and the other in Shiba Atagoshita. The liaison office was transferred to the latter. Taichirō, who was busier than ever, had to go out almost daily, and so he arranged for me to join my father at the Kōbusho. Shirō joined us not long after.

At the camp, I had no one my age to play with. Even though I was much younger than the others, I began studying with the older students at a school temporarily set up by Isawa Seijirō. We studied the Chinese classics, but again we merely read the passages aloud with no explanation. To supplement this, I took lessons with the scholar Satō Bigyokuken (real name Chūta) and read the *Analects*.

The prisoners at the camp were given a daily ration of four *gō* of rice and two hundred copper pennies.* Each month, on the days ending in one and six, we lined up in a room formerly used for sword practice and received our rice ration from contract merchants. The cooking was left to us, and each unit was provided with a small charcoal stove and an earthenware pot. The cooking responsibilities in my unit fell to me. I was warned that the rice, which was the short-grained Southeast Asian variety, required a certain cooking technique, but the kind of rice made no difference to me because I knew next to nothing about cooking. In a matter of days, however, I had learned how to make a decent pot of rice.

Taichirō often came by to talk to my father about recent developments. He also consulted with him in worried tones about my future. It evidently pained him to see me blithely going about chores, cooking rice and drawing water from the well. After several inquiries, he was able to persuade Hayashi

*One *gō* is approximately three-fourths of a cup, or 0.18 liters.

Shōjūrō (later Hayashi Kinji), an acquaintance in Numazu, to take me on as a student. Since I did not know where Numazu was, I felt somewhat apprehensive, but my father was delighted and did his best to cheer me up. On the eve of my planned escape, however, several prisoners escaped, and security was suddenly tightened. To my keen disappointment, I was unable to leave.

My brother continued his efforts, and toward the end of the year [1869], Yamauchi Kumanoshin, a samurai acquaintance, arranged for me to live as a working student at the house of a Tosa official, Mōri Kyōsuke. On the night of the twenty-seventh of the twelfth month, I went with Taichirō and Shirō to the northwest corner of the camp. We made our way in the dark, concealing ourselves behind a fence that ran along the Suidōbashi side of the river, and slipped out unnoticed. We kept walking until we reached the Ginza, chanced upon a beef shop, and ate a hearty farewell dinner.

I stayed the night with Taichirō at his lodgings at Tokusui-in, a subtemple of Zōjōji. My brother helped me gather my clothes together. As he showed me how to put on a *hakama**
and short sword, he said, "You realize that for Aizu, Tosa is a former enemy. I've even heard that Itagaki Taisuke was one of the commanding officers at the time of the siege of the castle. So no matter what happens, you are not to behave dishonorably." The sword, which bore the signature of the swordsmith Sōshū Tsunahiro, had probably belonged to an Aizu samurai. It has been my treasured possession ever since. Long afterward, I asked Viscount Matsudaira Yorihira, the curator of the sword collection at the Imperial Household Ministry, for an appraisal. He said that the sword was the work of an expert swordsmith and ranked with the best.

The following morning, I went with Taichirō to Yamauchi Kumanoshin's house near Ryōgokubashi. I said good-bye to my brother and spent the night at Yamauchi's house. The next day, he took me to the Tosa domain residence at Kajibashi Gate.

*A *hakama* is a divided skirt with pleats, which is worn over a kimono.

Mōri Kyōsuke lived in one of the small houses adjoining the main gate.

At the entrance, Yamauchi called out to the attendant: "Would you inform your master that I've brought the errand boy he asked me to find?" "Errand boy"—was that what I was supposed to be? I was deeply offended and tempted to leave on the spot. But then I thought of my father and Taichirō, and, swallowing my pride, I decided to stay.

I was shown to a room inside. I bowed politely and made my formal greetings to Mōri. It was the first time in my life that I had ever spoken to someone from another domain. Before leaving, Yamauchi said, "Beginning today, you will be employed in this house as a working student. Do whatever your master says." Two days later, I saw in the New Year [1870] at Mōri's house. I was now twelve.

The inner rooms of the house were occupied by Mōri, his mistress, Oshige, and her personal maid. The rooms to the front were for the use of Okamoto Sahei, who acted as steward, a younger man about seventeen or eighteen named Kaji, and three grooms called Bunkichi, Zenkichi, and Matsunosuke. In their company, I now entered a new phase of my life. I was by far the youngest and understood not a word of the Tosa dialect.

I soon discovered that I was a student in name only and really a common servant. Okamoto alone treated me like a samurai son. The others, unable to understand my accent, made me the butt of their jokes. The grooms, in particular, seemed to delight in shocking me with stories about gambling and indecent behavior.

My daily chores consisted of cleaning the rooms and receiving visitors at the front door. I also had to accompany Mōri whenever he went out on official business, since the other attendant, Kaji, was training to be a bugler for the Tosa domain forces and was away at practice all day. I had never done work of this nature, and, with determination, I obeyed Mōri's every wish. When I accompanied him on business, I had to wear my *hakama*, short sword, and a black cotton *haori* with the Mōri crest, the sleeves of which had been shortened to fit me. Mōri

was tall, and I, barely twelve, was small, and so when we walked outside, I had to scamper after him like a puppy. One time, when we were out on the street, he told me to straighten his *haori* collar. I stood on my tiptoes and tried jumping up to reach, but finally had to ask him to stoop over.

As a liaison official of his domain, Mōri went out every day. His work sometimes took him to the Dajōkan [Supreme Council], which was then located inside the Nijūbashi Gate. I would wait for him at the entrance, by a sign marked "Administrative Offices" just past the second approach to the gate. This is near what is now the palace parking ground. I also accompanied him to various domain offices, the homes of acquaintances, restaurants, teahouses, and the like. Along with the other, older attendants, I waited in the antechamber, but for me this was extremely distasteful because all they did was tell filthy stories or grab hold of the maidservants and tease them.

Going out with Mōri on rainy or snowy nights was also hard. I would have to run ahead of my long-legged master while holding a lantern at his feet to light his way in the dark. Even more irksome was accompanying him when he went out on his horse. Mōri, who was very fond of riding, kept three horses. One was a large, dappled Western horse, a rarity in those days. He would mount this particular horse, bid one of the grooms to go ahead of him, and have me run at his side. Immediately left behind, I would lose sight of him. Then I would have to elbow my way through the crowded streets and ask in my Aizu dialect whether anyone had seen a horse. This was a truly miserable experience. Once in a while, Mōri would notice this and wait for me to catch up. But on the days he reported to the Dajōkan, he would no sooner ride out of the Tosa Kajibashi residence than quickly break into a canter. Then he would gallop straight to the signpost at the Nijūbashi Gate, where all visitors had to dismount. He would wait there and laugh as I ran up, too out of breath to speak. Together, as master and attendant, we would go through the gate in proper form. He may have been amused by this, but I thought it heartless to tease someone so young.

Within two months or so I had formed a general idea of the location of various domain offices. I could go on errands on my own, understand the Edo dialect, and even reproduce it reasonably well. But in the course of sharing close quarters with the servants, I had become used to their lewd conversations and even started to take an interest in them. Worse yet, during the long hours I spent waiting until dawn in geisha houses and other establishments of ill repute, I learned about the highly irregular ways of the demimonde. I shudder to think of this now.

I remember one particular incident. I had accompanied Mōri to a restaurant called the Uricha and was waiting as usual in the antechamber when I received a message to go to his room. A lively party was in progress, and amid the geisha and guests, Mōri sat leaning against the alcove post. His face was flushed with drink.

"See this errand boy," he said for all to hear. "He's the son of an Aizu samurai, and because of the war, his mother and sisters all committed suicide." The women set aside their samisen and came up to me to murmur words of sympathy. I was furious. He had brought up the deaths of my loved ones for the sole amusement of his guests. What did he me take me for—a fool? I choked back the tears but was seething with rage as I excused myself and left the room.

Every ten days, the servants of the house, including Okamoto, were given money to buy some small food items from a vendor who came three times a day. I was given a silver one-*bu* coin, and would use the change left over from my purchases for such items as clogs, straw sandals, cotton hand towels, and for going to the public bathhouse.[7] Otherwise I received no pay.

Speaking of bathhouses, there was no bath at the house, though Mōri was a liaison official and of a respectable social status. Like everyone else in the neighborhood, he went to the public bathhouse inside the Kajibashi Gate. I had to accompany him there as well. I remember the first time we went. We entered the changing room upstairs, which was for the better

customers, and assuming that I would go in with him, I started to take off my *hakama*. "No," he said, "you stay here and watch my clothes." In the end, I went home without taking a bath.

It was now the fourth month of Meiji 3 [1870]. My situation at Mōri's house had not improved. I went to see Taichirō, and on his advice, decided to leave service. I would make up an excuse about how my father was ill and I was going to join him at the Kōbusho. I returned to Mōri's house ten days later, but as he was away in Tosa, I spoke to his mistress, Oshige, and expressed my thanks. She gave me a silver one-*bu* coin as a parting gift and told me to buy sweets for my father. I was caught in the rain at Kandabashi, however, and used the money to buy an umbrella.

Several years later, in Meiji 6 [1873], about the time I entered the Army Cadet School, I happened to be passing through Kōjimachi San-chōme when I noticed a house with Mōri's name on the front plaque. I decided to pay him a call. He was out, so I told his family what I had been doing lately and left my calling card. I made no further attempt to see him, though I vaguely remember hearing that he became a chamberlain to the Emperor Meiji and then governor of Shizuoka Prefecture but spent his last years in obscurity. About fifty years after this, a man by the name of Mōri Kujūrō came to see me. After introducing himself as a member of the Tachikawa City Assembly and Mōri Kyōsuke's son and heir, he asked me to write an epitaph for a memorial stone he planned for his father. I declined.

As I mentioned, the daimyo of Aizu had been officially pardoned and given a 30,000-*koku* domain in Mutsu Province. The daimyo house was thus spared from extinction, but once it became clear that the land could not support 4,000 samurai families, the men were told they were free to do as they wished. In the end, 210 families decided to return to Aizu, 500 to engage in farming or trade, 300 to settle in Edo or move elsewhere, 200 to go to Hokkaido, and the remaining 2,800 to accompany the daimyo to the new domain. My father and

Taichirō decided to go to Mutsu. In the meantime, Taichirō, as always concerned about my education, approached Kanda Takahira, the former *bakufu* scholar of Western learning [but nothing came of it].

On the seventeenth of the fourth month, we happened to hear that an imperial review was being held at Komaba (now Ikejiri-chō in Setagaya). Taichirō and I went to see it, and just as we neared the foot of what is now the Ōhashi Bridge, we caught a glimpse of the emperor, who was returning to the palace. His Majesty was astride his horse and arrayed in full warrior regalia. Flanking him were several sumo wrestlers, who held aloft two imperial banners emblazoned with the sun and moon. We watched until the procession passed from view, but Taichirō said not a word, nor did I ask him any questions.

Journey to Hell

Preparations for the move were finished, and in the middle of the fifth month [1870], we received orders to go to Mutsu Province. The new domain was made up of Ninohe, Sannohe, and Kita—three counties that had been confiscated from the Nanbu domain for siding with the *bakufu* in the war. It was to be called Tonami, or "south of Hokuto," after a line in an ancient Chinese poem: "Every land south of Hokuto [Ursa Major] comes under imperial rule." In Japan, too, the domains south of Hokkaido belonged to the emperor. Aizu was no exception; though removed to the far north, it was still a part of the emperor's realm and had in no sense been expelled.

My father said he wished to visit the family grave before making the trip north and left for Aizu alone. He would take the land route and join us in Tonami. Gosaburō and Shirō, thinking of the future, said they would remain in Tokyo and pursue their studies.

Along with about two hundred passengers, Taichirō and I took a barge from Shiodome to Shinagawa Bay, where we boarded an American ship. The ship, an eight-hundred-ton steamboat, was propelled by a pair of big paddle wheels and moved slowly. Inside the dark and cramped cabins, the passengers were squeezed together "like rice grains in a sushi roll." Since we came from a mountain country, we were at first excited by the prospect of a sea voyage, but as we sailed farther out,

we became more subdued. Before long, most of the passengers took to their beds, too sick even to sip water. I was the sickest of all, and was teased for looking more dead than alive.

One of the passengers onboard was a man who went by the name Miyagi Shūtarō. He was a scholar of Chinese studies in the Sendai domain, whose real name was Kurosawa Kamenoshin. For some reason he had gone into hiding at the An'yō-in, a subtemple at Zōjōji, and sought Taichirō's help to join our group.

The ship made a leisurely advance north, seeking shelter at fishing ports in rough weather, threading through coastal islands in high winds, all the while churning up water and spewing smoke. Finally, we rounded the Shimokita Peninsula and entered the choppy waters of Mutsu Bay. By the time we reached Noheji, our destination, more than half of the sixth month had passed.

The people who arrived ahead of us had separated into two groups, one settling in Noheji, and the other in Tanabu (now the city of Mutsu). A domain office was already in operation in Tanabu, with Yamakawa Ōkura as head officer. There was also a branch office in Noheji, headed by Kurasawa Uhei. We were lodged in a room at the home of Shimatani Seigorō, a local clothier.

The residents welcomed their new daimyo and his family with great warmth and courtesy. Our own host paid special attention to our meals, making sure that we were served delicacies from both land and sea. We had not eaten so well since leaving Aizu. In ten days or so, we moved to a temple called Kaichūji and shared quarters with four or five other families. The meals, alas, followed the Buddhist dietary regimen.

My father joined us toward the end of the seventh month. I was so happy to see him that I neglected to greet him in the proper manner and received a scolding from my brother. Taichirō by then had made up his mind to live permanently in Tonami and assist in its development. He married Sumi, the younger sister of Hinata Shinroku, a maternal relative, and began work as one of Kurasawa's assistants at the domain

branch office. There was no school, so I passed the time with my new friends, splashing about in the sea and a nearby river. I also went on an outing with Taichirō to a hot spring named Makado.

Since coming to Tonami my father had become even more taciturn. He kept to himself most of the time, preferring to fish at the river. Hunched over his rod, rigid and inert, he looked like a wooden statue, an image made of stone. With his eyes fixed on the water, he seemed to have forgotten to fish, indeed, to have forgotten his own self.

Summer lengthened into autumn, and as the leaves turned color and mushrooms ripened we felt a definite chill in the air. The old scholar Kurosawa, who lived with us, folded up his mosquito net and used it to cover himself at night. Everyone else, including my father, had no bedding at all and shivered in the cold.

In the ninth month, we were told to move from Noheji to Tanabu. We loaded what possessions we had on two packhorses and traveled up the coast, Sumi and I riding in turn. We passed through the port of Arito and spent the night at Yokohama, a village some fourteen miles away [from Noheji]. The next day we continued along the trackless coastline. A wild profusion of pale purple chamomile and red-berried sweetbrier stretched as far as the eye could see. Water tumbled down the cliffs, tossed by the sea breeze and sparkling in the brilliant sun. In Tanabu, Yamamoto Keizō, a prosperous local merchant, kindly arranged for us to stay temporarily with a fellow merchant called Sakamoto. Shortly after, we rented a house in Mukōmachi from a man called Kudō Rinzō.

By this time the domain's rice supply was running dangerously low. Though the assessment was 30,000 *koku*, the actual product was closer to 7,000, an amount clearly inadequate to feed the samurai population. After a consultation, the domain leaders sent Taichirō to Hakodate to negotiate the purchase of rice with the resident Danish consul, Burikisuton.[8] Taichirō succeeded in purchasing the rice, but then Yonekura, the merchant acting as broker, ran away with the money. The Danish consul

[having handed over the rice] demanded that our domain compensate him. Fearing that the domain would suffer, Taichirō took responsibility for the affair. The consul, however, insisted that the domain was responsible, and presented his case to the government in Tokyo. Taichirō was arrested and sent under guard to Tokyo. Thanks to my brother's sense of honor and duty, the domain had been saved from paying out huge sums of money. The men at the Justice Ministry, who were informed about the situation, fully sympathized with Taichirō. Although there was the possibility of protracted negotiations [with a foreign power], they cited extenuating circumstances and imposed a light prison sentence. In all this, I felt especially sorry for Sumi. Separated from her husband so soon after her marriage, she was to spend the next seven years waiting patiently in Tonami with her father-in-law.

In Tonami, our daily rations consisted of three *gō* of unpolished rice for adults and two *gō* for children. We were also given 200 *mon* to cover clothing, shelter, and all other expenses. Many families found themselves unable to pay the rent and left one by one for the wilderness. Naming one such site Tonamigaoka, they put up thatched huts no larger than eighteen to twenty-four feet square and set to work reclaiming the land. In our own family, Taichirō, the most able-bodied member, was in Tokyo, and so we decided to stay in Kudō's house until the spring.

The house we rented had originally been built as a shop. It had a frontage about eighteen feet wide, a room on the second floor the size of six mats, and on the first floor, a ten-mat-size room with a hearth for cooking.* Behind the house was a storage shed. The rooms had no tatami flooring, and the indoor partitions lacked paper panels. To fend off the cold, we spread reed mats on the floor, covered the frames of the partitions with old rice sacks, and built a fire in the hearth. Still, the north wind from Mutsu Bay swept into the room, and even near the hearth,

*In Japan, rooms are measured by the number of tatami mats they can accommodate. One mat is about three by six feet.

the temperature hovered between ten and fifteen degrees below zero [Celsius]. The rice gruel we cooked often froze solid as a rock, and before meals, we first had to thaw it out. Our clothes kept us from freezing to death, but since I was young and had little resistance, I soon came down with a fever. The fever persisted through the winter months for forty days. I had no bedding of any sort and simply burrowed deeper into my straw sack.

My father spent the time sitting by the hearth making fishnets and trying his hand at other newly acquired skills. My sister-in-law Sumi earned extra money weaving all day at a training center that had been set up to encourage cottage industries. The firewood we had collected in the autumn soon ran out, and we tramped in the deep snow looking for dead branches. For charcoal, we used the burnt remains of firewood, and to heat our foot warmers, we made briquettes with leftover ashes—a difficult and time-consuming task. Needless to say, buying such items was beyond our means.

Our only source of water was the Tanabu River, some 250 yards away. In the winter, we bored a hole in the frozen surface and hauled the water with a bucket. We three took turns carrying the bucket, but to our dismay, we would find the surface frozen by the time we got home and would have to melt it. We milled our ration of rice at a neighbor's house, and supplementing this with soybeans, potatoes, and whatever else we could get, made a thin gruel. Luxuries such as plain white rice or white rice gruel were beyond our fondest dreams. When potatoes were unavailable, we collected *konbu*, *wakame*, and other seaweed that had washed ashore. We spread these out to dry, pounded the pieces into tiny chips with a stick, and cooked them with the gruel. The chips, which were called "*oshime*" by the local inhabitants, had apparently seen them through many a famine. Dullish brown, with a sharp, pungent smell, they had a very unpleasant taste.

For vegetables, we gathered the plants that grew wild in the surrounding mountains and fields. During the winter months, we were forced to eat salted beans day after day. My father

thought he would try making tofu and went to great trouble to crush the boiled soybeans, but he finally had to give up. Of course, we had neither sugar nor soy sauce.[9] But even in the winter, we could dig out the roots of bracken from under the snow. These we pounded and washed repeatedly in a vat of water until the starch sank to the bottom. We then mixed the starch with rice bran, added salt, and made dumplings, which we threaded on a skewer and toasted over the fire. They were almost tasteless, and as we ate them, we kept saying how nice it would be to have just a little sugar.

The first winter, it was all we could do not to perish from cold or hunger. With inadequate nutrition, we steadily lost weight and showed symptoms of beriberi. This made enduring the piercing cold even more difficult.

Toward the end of winter, the Tanabu River had begun to thaw. A hunter came by and shot a dog that was playing on the ice floes behind the Entsūji Temple, but as the ice was dangerously thin, he had left the carcass behind. We knew the dog belonged to a blacksmith who lived on the other side of the Tanabu Bridge, and after giving the matter some thought, my father ordered me to go quickly to the owner and ask for the carcass. I ran in the slushy snow, told the blacksmith what had happened, and obtained his permission.

Just as I reached home, a middle-aged samurai who lived in one of the huts in Tonamigaoka came running over. He said that he had gone this minute to the blacksmith to ask for the dog but had been told it was promised to the Shiba family and that he would have to negotiate with us. In return for half of the carcass, he added, he would risk walking on the ice. My father smiled ruefully and gave his consent. The man returned, dragging the carcass. He took it apart in the shed and went off with his share.

Dogmeat now became part of our daily diet. It was delicious, even boiled in saltwater with no additional seasoning. The dog had been big. Though my father and I ate the meat every day, there was still some left to consume. Sumi, from the start, refused to touch it, saying the mere sight made her queasy.

But as far as I was concerned, the meat was no mere side dish but food that filled a basic need in my diet.

One day, however, I reached my limit. I was unable to swallow the piece in my mouth and suddenly felt nauseous. My father noticed this. "Have you forgotten you are the son of a samurai? In war, when soldiers run out of food, they'll eat cats, dogs, anything to keep on fighting. We came to this miserable, forsaken wilderness because we were hounded by the enemy. If those scoundrels from Satsuma and Chōshū ever hear that the Aizu samurai have died of starvation, they'll ridicule us. Our domain will go down in infamy. This is a battlefield, do you hear? It's a battlefield until the day Aizu wipes the stain from its honor."

My father, who was usually soft-spoken, had scolded me with unexpected vehemence. I was taken aback; trembling, I closed my eyes and swallowed the meat in one gulp. I choked and sputtered. Looking at me, my father put his chopsticks down and said, "I think we've had enough for today."

My father and I ate the meat for twenty days straight. Perhaps because of this or because of the lack of nutrition in general, my hair began falling out that spring, and soon I became as bald as a Buddhist bonze.

The Fight against Famine

It is the children's duty to see to their parents' every comfort. In the winter, the children are to fill up the crevices in their parents' room, keep the fire burning in the hearth, pay particular attention to their food, and serve warm dishes. In the summer, they are to remove all partitions between the rooms to let the air circulate, sprinkle the ground with cooling water, burn incense sticks to keep away mosquitoes, and arrange the bedding so that their parents may enjoy a good night's rest. Children in houses with many servants are to instruct them well in these matters. Also, each morning, the children are to go to their parents' room and inquire after their health. Should they find their parents still in bed, they are to urge them gently and in a pleasing manner to continue to rest. They should then quietly withdraw.

Such were the teachings in the *Dōjikun*, the textbook we studied as children in Aizu. But living as we did in a beggar's hovel and reduced to eating dogmeat, I could not put a single precept into practice. To tell the truth, I had long since relegated these teachings to the back of my mind, and only now, startled by my father's harsh rebuke, did I think of them. My father had said this place of exile was a battlefield, and so it would be until we avenged ourselves on the enemy. Yet what was I but the hapless son of a ruined samurai, a son now accustomed to his lowly station in life? I felt sorry for myself, though as I look back, I realize that it must have been even more painful for my

father, who was put into the position of scolding me and forc-
ing me to eat dogmeat.

Our house was at the far end of Tanabu, where the town
had given way to fields. In autumn, peasants passed by, leading
packhorses piled high with the new crop of white radishes. As
soon as they came into view, the local women and children
would dash out from both sides of the street, snatch a couple of
radishes, and run off. The peasants, who never tried to stop
them, would just hurry on. Impoverished and hungry, the Aizu
people looked on in envy, but I am proud to say that not one
person stooped to petty thievery.

The young daimyo Kataharu, who was barely three, lived
at the Entsūji Temple. His father, Katamori, lived with him,
nominally in his custody. My father went to see them from time
to time, taking gifts of wild chives and bracken or fish he had
caught in the river. On these visits, he would be received by the
young daimyo, who was accompanied by women attendants.
My father would be given some sweets—little cakes made of
bracken-root paste and sprinkled with roasted soybean powder.
My father always brought these home, and he, Sumi, and I ate
them together, savoring each bite.

The domain office was housed in what was formerly the
office of a district official of the Nanbu domain. As vice-gover-
nor,* Yamakawa Ōkura drew a meager monthly salary of three
ryō. Struggling to feed his family, he secretly arranged with the
local tofu dealer to buy up all the dregs.† Word of this leaked
out, and several men representing the samurai took him to task
and made him abandon this arrangement.

A school for children was opened in the main hall of Entsū-
ji, with Isawa Seijirō as headmaster. Instead of the traditional
texts, such as the *Book of Filial Piety* and the *Analects*, we now
read books by Fukuzawa Yukichi: *All the Countries of the*

*After the Restoration, daimyo were named *han chiji*, or governors of their
domains, but the actual power was held by samurai vice-governors (*daisanji*), who
headed the domain administration.

†Tofu dregs (*okara*) were traditionally used to feed livestock. The contention
over the tofu dregs is an indication of the severe shortage of food and money.

World (Sekai kunizukushi), *Conditions in the West* (Seiyō jijō), and *Illustrated Science Primer* (Kyūri zukai).* Looking back, this was a significant change, for ever since the Hōei 5 [1708] prohibition of "teachings other than those of Confucius, Mencius, and Chu Hsi," children in Aizu had been educated solely in the Chu Hsi interpretation—even to the exclusion of the school of ancient learning [a competing school that emphasized a return to the original Confucian texts]. Thus, after 160 years [of orthodoxy], education in Aizu was liberated.

I went to school every morning and also took lessons in the Chinese classics with Kurosawa Kamenoshin, the old scholar from Sendai. In the afternoons, I played with about thirty boys inside the compound of the Jigentarō Myōjin Shrine. The boys were mostly from low-ranking families, who lived outside the castle precincts. They did not know that calling one's peers by surname only was accepted practice at the Nisshinkan and was not considered rude. Offended when I dropped the usual honorary suffixes, they accused me of insulting them and bullied me whenever they could.

It was about this time that the Ariga family, the in-laws of one of my great-aunts, made repeated requests to adopt me as their heir. [My father asked me about this, but] I refused.

The long winter was over at last. We had survived; we were still alive, and in a grateful state of mind, we welcomed the first warm days of the fourth year of Meiji [1871]. Earlier on, my father and Taichirō had decided to settle permanently on land near the Arakawa River, where it flowed by the foot of Mount Kamafuse. Unfortunately, Taichirō was sent to jail and the plan was abandoned, but with the coming of spring, my father resolved to go ahead on his own. If we did not take advantage of the planting season, we would be faced yet again with starvation. But we needed a place to live, and again, with the help of the merchant Yamamoto Keizō, we rented part of a house in Otoshinosawa that was owned by Nitta Hatsugorō.

*Fukuzawa Yukichi (1835–1901) was an educator and leading proponent of the adoption of Western learning. His books were read widely by the general public.

We hired a small boat, packed it with our meager posses-
sions, and traveled down the Tanabu River. Though the ice had
melted, the banks were still covered with deep snow. We went
ashore at an isolated spot upstream from the village of Hidoro-
da. Shouldering our belongings, we made our way through a
mile or so of dense bamboo thickets.

The village of Otoshinosawa had only two houses—the
house owned by our landlord and another belonging to a relat-
ed family, who lived about a hundred yards downriver. The
closest village, Hidoroda, was about two-thirds of a mile away
and had fourteen houses. Ōhira, the next closest, was a mile
and a half away. Two and a half miles farther off was the vil-
lage of Kanaya. In the far distance loomed Osorezan, the
famous mountain abode of shamans and mediums. There were
forests of pines and other trees, and near the lower slopes, a
scattering of rice fields. It was a place of utter desolation, bleak
and inhospitable, where even woodcutters and hunters seldom
came. Here no barking dogs could be heard, and the silence was
broken only by the yelping of foxes, the chatter of wild birds,
the wind blowing through the pine forests, and the rain beating
down on the thickets. Our landlord had planted some peach
trees near the house, and as we gazed at this rare sight, we won-
dered aloud if in the spring, the house would turn into a veri-
table "Peach Blossom Spring," the rural utopia imagined by the
Chinese poet Ta'o Ch'ien.

A peach blossom utopia in the spring, perhaps, but what
we confronted now were our dismal living quarters—a four-
mat-size room with a bare wooden floor, which we covered
with straw and reed mats, and an eight-mat room, similarly
bare, with a large hearth in the center about three by six feet.
At one end of the second room stood a row of shelves, and at
the other end, a wooden wall that separated us from the land-
lord's living quarters. As in the previous house, the frames of
the indoor partitions had no paper in the panels. The privy out-
side in the shed was a dubious affair made of two planks bal-
anced across a wooden barrel that had been sunk into the
ground. For light, we relied on the glow of the hearth fire or

burned the roots of pine trees; lamp oil was unheard of. The villagers were apparently not in the habit of taking baths. In warmer weather, they bathed in the river, but in the winter, they had no way to wash themselves.

Most of the local men worked in the fisheries in Hokkaido to earn extra money and returned during the winter months to prepare for the planting season. This and other pieces of information convinced my father that it was none too soon to start preparing for the coming winter. The three of us set to work clearing the land. Meanwhile, the domain had been experimenting with smelting iron sand, which was readily available, and had already begun to produce spades, hoes, and other tools for distribution. We made use of these implements as we dug up the bracken that covered the ground, brought the plants home, washed off the dirt after a sizable amount had been accumulated, and then removed the leaves. We then spread the roots on a rack about six feet square that we had borrowed from the landlord and pounded them with a stick until they turned into a glutinous, pasty mass. We put this into a wooden vat, about two by six feet and shaped like a dugout canoe. We poured in water and scooped out the fibers and other foreign matter that floated to the top. We also rocked the vat periodically to remove the finer particles with a sieve. Then we repeated the process, changing the water each time. Left to rest overnight, the starch would sink to the bottom and coagulate. We scraped this starch out with a scallop shell, rinsed it in water repeatedly, and let it dry. The final product was a white, powdery substance. With three people working, we averaged about one and a half quarts of starch a day, and on good days, as much as two and a quarter. When put up for sale in Tanabu, one and a half quarts fetched 200 *mon*.

Our next task was to weed and plow the soil we had cleared of bracken. This much we could do. But when it came to growing vegetables, we were complete novices. Scarcely would the beans and leafy green vegetables grow to a certain height than the insects would devour them. Our rice field, which was no larger than 150 square feet, yielded absolutely nothing. Because

the landlord's fields bordered ours, we thought we would just
follow his example, but all we produced was a bunch of stringy
radishes and a handful of shriveled potatoes.

Our main diet was the same watery gruel mixed in with dry
seaweed chips. Every so often, the landlord would bring over a
couple of bowls of millet gruel—delicious, as I remember—or a
dish of *awa* dumplings, lightly salted and covered with millet
sauce. We were unsuccessful in growing vegetables, but at least
in summer we could pick parsley, butterbur, and chives to our
heart's content. Firewood was also plentiful, as was wild mul-
berry. We picked the leaves and carried as many as we could to
Tanabu, where we sold them for one *namisen* coin, then the
equivalent of twenty-four *mon*. It was not much, but enough to
pay for a visit to the bathhouse.

Since moving to Otoshinosawa I had stopped attending the
school in Tanabu and spent each day digging up the soil. My
former teacher, Isawa Seijirō, came by one day to urge me to
resume my studies. I was deeply touched by his kindness, but
felt I could not leave all the work to my father and Sumi.

Late in the spring, my brother Gosaburō arrived unexpect-
edly from Tokyo. My father was taken aback but overjoyed to
see him. Gosaburō had remained in Tokyo with the intention of
becoming a seaman, but the *Ando Maru*, the domain ship on
which he was training, had foundered off Bōsō Bay. On going
ashore, he had heard of Taichirō's imprisonment in connection
with the rice money, abandoned his plans, and hastened to
Tonami.

My brother was aghast at our living conditions, and the
very next day started helping my father. He was also distressed
to see that I had given up my studies and become an ordinary
peasant boy. He arranged to have me live in Tanabu with his
friend Kobayashi Hidemori so that I could go back to school. I
moved into Kobayashi's house in the sixth month, and on
school holidays—the days ending in one or six—I returned
home to collect my five days' ration of rice that had accumu-
lated. My only chore at Kobayashi's house was to cook meals,
so I had plenty of time to study.

At the approach of summer, we were pestered by mosqui-
toes. No one in the house, not even Kobayashi, owned a mos-
quito net. The other lodgers and I finally got some wood shav-
ings from a sawyer and burned these by our bedside at night.

Autumn came and went; the dread winter was upon us
again. With only the straw mats we had put up the year before,
the house remained mercilessly exposed to the wind that blew
in from Mutsu Bay. At night the ice blue rays of the moon
streamed into the house, while far off, foxes kept up their
melancholy cry. The sleet would sometimes splatter in through
the crevices in the wall, the crinkling sound intensifying the bit-
ter cold. Even with the fire going all day, we were never warm.
If you sat with your back to the fire, your front would ache
with the cold; if you faced the fire, your back tingled. Our
hands were always numb, and to bring back the circulation, we
held them over the fire and rubbed them together. As a result of
a lack of nutrition and the hours we spent braiding straw rope
in winter, our skin became as rough as the straw itself.

We resigned ourselves to yet another winter in our hovel.
Buffeted by the north wind and huddled near the hearth, we
wrapped ourselves in our straw mats like so many bagworms.*
But Gosaburō was to be pitied the most, for saying he felt it was
improper to sleep under the same roof as his brother's wife
while his brother was absent, he had moved to a small Inari
shrine in a grove about 120 yards away. None of us had quilts,
but at least we had the warmth of a fire. Deprived even of this,
he spent the night bundled in his straw sacks and mats. When
he came over in the morning, he would find the tracks of foxes,
rabbits, mice, and other foraging animals around the shrine and
house.

It began to snow heavily, and making the trip home every
fifth day became increasingly arduous. I had been without clogs
or straw sandals for some time and had gone about in my bare
feet, washing them in a bucket of water before entering the

*Bagworms, or larvae of moths of the family Psychidae, are encased in
cocoons covered with dry twigs and leaves.

house. But now, with the temperature frequently plunging to fifteen below zero, my feet would stick to the icy snow and get frostbitten; I either had to keep stamping my feet or run as fast as I could. Even so, I would often lose all sensation in my feet, and in alarm, I would rush into the Miyake home in Kanaya to warm them briefly. I would then run full speed on the snow-clogged path with my thin summer clothes flapping in the wind. Once home, I would get my share of the rice ration from my father and dash off, retracing the road to Tanabu. My father and Gosaburō tried in vain to make some sort of covering for my feet. Unable to bear the cold, I went to my Noguchi aunt to ask if I could borrow some footwear. She said she had none to spare.

Sometime in the middle of winter, I was told to give up my studies and come home. I was given no explanation and wondered if Kobayashi had said something to my brother. Accompanied by my brother, I returned to the house in the wilderness.

The fields and mountains were blanketed with snow. We were unable to dig bracken roots and spent the days braiding rope with the straw we unraveled from old rice sacks. With no books at hand, studying was out of the question. The family had come to Mutsu with high hopes, little knowing the land was so barren and unforgiving. But at this point, it was useless to complain or give in to anger; we could only endure our fate.

I imagine it was particularly hard on Sumi. Although they had been poor, she and Taichirō had just begun a new life as husband and wife when Taichirō was sent to jail. His day of release was unknown. Had the times been different, she would have led a life of privilege. Free from mundane cares, she would have devoted herself to flower arrangement, the tea ceremony, the koto, poetry, and other social graces. But now, she did not even have cloth to mend her clothes, to say nothing of oil to smooth her hair. For that matter, we were all a sorry sight—faces gaunt, hair unkempt, hands and feet chapped. Slurping watery gruel to stave off hunger, we had become a family of beggars.

We braided rope from morning until night, shivering as the

north wind whipped the straw mats hanging on the door frames. When our fingers became stiff, we tried to concentrate harder, forcing all our strength into our fingertips. As we silently worked, I thought about what had become of us. Was this what they called the "special largess" awarded us to revive the domain? Was this what they called the "ever-unchanging imperial benevolence" toward Aizu, the gesture of grace and favor that had so moved our samurai to tears of joy? Was that indeed how they saw our fate? Let me be absolutely candid and say that this was not the revival of the domain nor an act of mercy: This was exile, pure and simple, and at no time in our nation's history had an entire domain been subjected to such cruel punishment.

Other thoughts ran through my mind. We had been treated most unjustly; even at my tender age, I could tell right from wrong. If this was to be our destiny, it was just as well that my grandmother, mother, and sisters had killed themselves; I myself would have been better off dying with them. Foolish thoughts, to be sure, but when I gazed into the hearth fire, I seemed to see the castle town engulfed in flames and the mutilated body of my mother cloaked in white silk. Tears ran down my cheeks.

It was too painful to recall the past; to lament the present served no purpose; to place our hopes in the future seemed equally futile. So while we may have worked side by side plaiting rope near the hearth, each of us retreated into a grim silence. There was no past or future, only the cold and hungry present, and that was what made our plight so hard to bear. Perhaps we would have found it easier to live each day preparing for death. I had been told repeatedly that death was but the final stage in life, and this surely was true. I had been told that life could be understood only when one was confronted with death, and this, too, was doubtless true. But in our present situation one could not even seek release in death. "Those scoundrels from Satsuma and Chōshū will make a mockery of us. Do you want them to say, 'Well, what do you know, those wretched Aizu samurai have finally starved to death in Shimokita.' We've got to stay alive, stay alive until we've vindi-

cated Aizu's honor. This place is a battlefield!" My father's words still rang in my ears, and I had not forgotten how, half retching, I had swallowed the piece of dogmeat.

"Don't die. Don't even think about it. Bear up—spring will come one day. Stay alive until you've taken revenge on those scoundrels." I scolded myself and tried to keep my spirits up, but for a young boy, constant hunger was hard. And so in silence, we braided rope, giving vent to our bitterness with each motion of our fingers; we would do the same the day after, and the day after that.

A Ray of Hope
in the Wilderness

But even in the wilderness, where famine stalked us and ravens croaked ominously all day, the morning sun did shine its bright rays down upon us. At the end of Meiji 4 [1871], sometime past the middle of the twelfth month, I unexpectedly received good news: I had been chosen by the Tonami administration to go to the Aomori prefectural office to work as an office boy and further my studies. Noda Hiromichi, the vice-governor of Aomori, had consented to take me under his wing. I was certain Gosaburō had used his connections to make this possible.

Earlier in the year, on the fourteenth of the seventh month, when the government abolished the domains and instituted the prefectural system, Tonami had become Tonami Prefecture. Hirosaki became Hirosaki Prefecture, with Noda Hiromichi, then twenty-eight, as vice-governor. Tonami and Hirosaki soon merged with several other prefectures to become Aomori Prefecture, and Noda, who was again named vice-governor, moved to the new prefectural office in Aomori City; he was thirty-one years old.

Noda was originally from the Kumamoto domain in Kyushu. He was the youngest brother of Ishimitsu Matami, the head of the office of domain products, and had been adopted by Noda [Junpei], who served in the financial magistrate's office. In the last years of *bakufu* rule, Noda [Hiromichi] stud-

ied in Kyoto with Yokoi Shōnan, the renowned scholar of the Jitsugaku school of Confucian studies. In later years, he entered the army, became the first director of its accounting office, and was made a baron. He was said to be a self-effacing man, with a strong sense of justice, and a generous mentor to younger men. He had been a commanding officer at the time of the siege of Hakodate, and so from our point of view was a former enemy, but was known to stand apart from the government clique dominated by Satsuma, Chōshū, Tosa, and Hizen and be particularly helpful to samurai sons from the northeastern domains. I decided to accept the offer—it was the chance of a lifetime.

Also chosen was Mori Toranosuke, the oldest son of Mori Hiromori. One year older than I, he was a brilliant student at the school in Tanabu. He later changed his name to Mori Masamori and reached the rank of major, but died while studying military affairs in Italy.

I should mention that when the domains were replaced by prefectures, the daimyo, who served briefly as prefectural governors, had all been relieved of their posts. In our domain, the young daimyo Kataharu and his father Katamori took the occasion to leave Tonami. They expressed their gratitude to the samurai for long years of loyal service during times of great hardship and departed for Tokyo on the twenty-fifth of the eighth month.* The samurai in Tonami were devastated. The work of developing the land had only begun. Bereft of their mainstay and support, they would have to fend for themselves. Aizu was no more; their dreams of restoring the domain to its former glory had dissipated like the morning fog; they were without status or office. What were they to do?

My family, too, had been cast down to the depths of despair. When the news of my selection came, we were jubilant. My father, scarcely able to contain his joy and yet too distracted to plait rope, walked around in a daze. My sister-in-law,

*The government ordered all daimyo to move to Tokyo.

however, promptly took down the storage box from the shelf and inspected my clothes to see if they required mending. It was the custom in samurai families to reserve a set of formal clothes for such contingencies, and I must confess that after all these months, my spirits lifted at the sight of my *haori* and *hakama*. I put on the *haori* and *hakama*, tucked my short sword into my waistband, and put on the straw sandals my father had hastily made. Accompanied by Gosaburō, I set off on the icy road, my heart joyous. For once, I did not feel the cold. Even the snow-covered mountains and fields, so familiar now, looked beautiful that day.

At the Tanabu office, I received verbal confirmation of my selection and warm words of encouragement from Vice-Governor Yamakawa, who was acting on behalf of the former daimyo. In retrospect, the meeting was like the imperial audiences granted to military officers sent abroad to study in early Meiji. I also received one *ryō* for travel expenses.

On the way home, I paid my respects to Yamamoto Keizō, the merchant who had kindly looked after us since our arrival. He gave me one *shu* as a going-away present. Back home, I gave a full account to my father. He was moved to tears and slipped a one-*bu* coin into an old purse that he had taken out. I now had a total of one *ryō*, one *bu*, and one *shu*.

My wardrobe was in order—an undergarment, padded *haori*, *hakama*, and short sword. I packed a change of underwear, a cotton hand towel, and tissue paper in a woven bamboo traveling case measuring about twenty-five by ten inches. This I secured tightly with a linen band. I put the money in the purse and hung it around my neck with a cord that I had attached to one end. I tucked the purse into the front of my kimono. When I was ready to leave, I sat in front of my father and bowed to the floor. I recited the lines my brother had taught me: "Father, I shall not return until I have made something of myself. I beg of you to wait for me in good health." My father nodded without a word. Sumi quietly wept.

Gosaburō accompanied me partway, and I left the village of

Otoshinosawa, tramping through the icy snow. Mori was waiting for me in Tanabu. We mounted a pair of packhorses supplied by the office and, led by two grooms, set out on our journey. Mori was then fourteen; I was thirteen.

Traveling was easy. The office had sent word ahead to the post stations to provide us with fresh horses and to handle sleeping accommodations. All expenses were borne by the local officials. We stayed the first night at an inn in Yokohama, a fishing village some fourteen miles from Tanabu. For our evening meal, we were given fish, vegetables, and soup. The meal was served on individual lacquer trays—something I had not seen for a while. The rice, a pure white, was another treat. I had not eaten white rice for so long that I had forgotten how delicious it was. Our bedding was also luxurious—quilts to sleep on, quilts to put on top. I paused for a minute or two before getting under the covers.

The next morning, we continued to Noheji, some fourteen miles farther along the coast. I remembered having taken the same route with my family the previous autumn, but now it was battered by icy gales and was extremely treacherous. People were known to lose their way in the blinding snow and freeze to death; not for nothing was the place called "Life's Last Journey," or "The Coast of Hell." Angry waves sent up clouds of spray, and the horses frequently lost their footing, as did the grooms when clumps of ice clung to their straw sandals. Luckily, we had been provided with pieces of bear hide and dog hide to shield ourselves from the wind. Because we had eaten well and enjoyed a good night's rest, we were warm, and the circulation in our feet and hands was normal. In fact, we were rather enjoying the trip.

The inn in Noheji was run by Kawarada, a samurai who used to live near us on Hon Sannochō. His son was a childhood friend, so we were given a hearty welcome. We took our ease around the brazier and exchanged news, sipping tea and nibbling sweets, just as if we were back in Aizu. Another friend, Kimura Yūjirō (later Osamu), lived in the area. He envied my

good fortune, and spurred by my example, later came to Aomori, went to Tokyo to study, and eventually became quite successful.

We left in the morning and stopped for our noon meal at a small port. Midway, I discovered that I had lost the purse my father had given me. I was frantic, but then one of the grooms, an honest soul, found it lying on the saddle and brought it over. We resumed our trip, but I began to doze and fell off the horse, perhaps because I had eaten too much. The snow had made the ground higher than usual, and I apparently caught my head in one of the branches of a tree. I was fortunately not hurt.

By the time we reached the village of Nonai, the sun had set, and on arriving at Aomori late at night, we went directly to the house where Kajiwara Heima, Noguchi Kurodayū, and other Aizu samurai who had become prefectural officials were staying. Vice-Governor Noda happened to be visiting, and as he was about to leave, we were introduced to him in the kitchen. He asked for my name and told me to come to his house at a later date.

We reported to the prefectural office the following morning. Kajiwara, the former Aizu elder who was in charge of general affairs, solemnly informed us that we had been appointed office attendants; our wages would be two *bu* a month.

For the next four or five days, we commuted to work from our inn. We rose early in the morning and ran the two-thirds of a mile of snow-covered road to get to the office before the others arrived. We first started a fire, boiled water, cleaned the rooms, filled the braziers with charcoal, and set the iron tea kettles in place. When we used water, bits of ice stuck to our fingers and crackled. Our chores finished, we raced back to the inn for breakfast, then flew back again to the office. Stray dogs loitered in our path; they barked and chased after us as soon as they saw we were children.

I was soon ordered to move to Noda's official residence and work as his personal attendant; I would continue to report to the office during the day. Living in the house was Maeno Eishirō, who worked for Noda and was from Maesawa; a policeman

from Aizu named Magara; a groom, Yoshizō, from Kumamoto; and a kitchen maid. Noda was still single, so the house seemed more like a student dormitory, with Noda acting as senior monitor. My friend Mori joined us before long.

Noda, as I mentioned, was known for helping out younger men; he did this not only as a matter of principle, but from genuine interest. Some of the more famous men he took under his patronage were Gotō Shinpei, Saitō Makoto, Hayashida Kametarō, and Takamichi Takeo.

The work at the office was not at all onerous; it was even pleasant. After all, Mori and I had lived like beggars in Tonami. Our reputation accordingly rose, and in time, all the attendants at the office were drawn from Aizu families. I noticed it made no difference to Noda whether one's family had been for the *bakufu* or against it; he judged people solely on the merits of their character. Under his influence, I found myself shedding some of my old biases and gaining a broader outlook on life.

A solemn ceremony was held at the prefectural office on New Year's Day [Meiji 5; 1872]. Noda appeared first, wearing traditional court dress of black lacquered *eboshi* cap and loose, flowing robe with wide sleeves and trailing hem. Then the other officials filed in, looking most impressive in formal attire of stiff linen upper garments and *hakama*. The ceremony was followed by a magnificent banquet. As I ate the food, I wished with all my heart that I could give even half my portion to my father in Tonami.

I saw my first Western-style lamp when Noda was entertaining at home one evening. Unfortunately, it failed to light. One day, I noticed some scallions at a vegetable shop. I had not seen them since leaving Aizu, so I purchased two bunches and sent them to my father by courier mail. I never heard whether they arrived safely or not. There was no mail service like the one we have now, and for all deliveries, including letters, we relied on these couriers.

I was given permission to go out in the evenings to take calligraphy and reading lessons from Sekiba Tadatake and a man called Satō. At the office, I continued to work diligently. My ini-

tial wages of two *bu* gradually rose, and by the time I left
Aomori in the sixth month, they had risen [fourfold] to two yen
a month. I spent part of my wages as pocket money and gave
the rest to Noda for safekeeping. The currency system had
changed in the meantime, and we now used paper notes in
denominations of one yen [one-half yen], twenty sen, and ten
sen. A mail service was also opened between Tokyo and
Aomori. Delivery was reliable and prompt, and everyone mar-
veled at how this could be done without relying on couriers.

Early in the year, the new governor, Hishida Bunzō, arrived
to take up his post, and my friend Mori was transferred to the
home of a member of his staff named Kuroda. Actually, the two
of us had been hoping to go to Tokyo at the first chance. As it
happened, Nasu Hitoshi, a finance ministry official who was
originally from the Kurobane domain, had come to Aomori on
business, so when I learned that he and Noda were on good
terms, I asked Noda if he would arrange for me to accompany
Nasu on his return trip to Tokyo. I also went to talk to Nasu
on my own. He said I could work for him as a servant on a trial
basis at his inn, the Kanazawaya. I worked very conscientious-
ly, but in a month or so, on the day before his departure, he said
that pressing duties prevented him from taking me. I probably
had failed to meet his standards.

Sometime later, a German warship sailed into Aomori.
Noda and his staff gave the crew a grand reception, and in
return, everyone, including the local residents, was invited to go
aboard and see the ship. When we had finished the tour, an offi-
cer remembered that I had served food during the reception and
invited me to his room and gave me some sweets. It was at this
moment that I conceived a bold plan: I would return the next
day, hide in a corner of the ship, and after it had put out to sea,
I would reveal myself and ask to be hired as a cabin boy. That
same evening, as I was walking along the shore with Noda, I
discovered to my dismay that the ship already had set sail and
was on the other side of Mutsu Bay. To this day, I can clearly
remember how disappointed I was.

Noda kept a mistress called Osono, and after a while he

moved her into the official residence. The weather warmed, and
the snow melted; the plum and cherry trees burst into bloom at
the same time, with the peonies quickly following. It was the
season for outings. I accompanied Noda to flower-viewing par-
ties, plays, shrine festivals, and the like, and mingled freely with
geisha and dancing girls. Spending money was fast becoming a
habit. I ordered a new kimono and *hakama*, and thought noth-
ing of buying food at outdoor stalls.

At the end of the fifth month, a delegation of finance min-
istry officials who were inspecting the land tax reform in the
northeast arrived in Aomori. The delegation was headed by
Nagaoka Shigehiro, a middle-level official who was from the
Ōmura domain in Hizen. Next in rank was Ichikawa Masaya-
su, who was from Shinshū Matsumoto, and then three subor-
dinates named Doi, Kitamura, and Yamada. Their visit could
not have come at a better moment. I decided to confide in Noda
about my hopes to study in Tokyo and asked if he would inter-
cede with the officials to take me with them. He approved of
my plans and suggested that I go and speak to them myself; he
would then take appropriate action. I went to the officials' inn
and told them about my hopes for the future.

"Have you any relatives in Tokyo?" one of the officials
asked. "Oh, yes, my brother Shirō is there, and there's a rela-
tive, Kimura Ushitoku. There are also my brother's friends—
Akizuki Teijirō, Kōsaka Munekiyo, Teshirogi Naoemon. Any
of these people would be willing to take care of me." I reeled
off a list of names that popped into my head. Of those I men-
tioned, Kimura was my eighteen-year-old nephew and an
impoverished student, but of course the men had no way of
knowing this. The officials seemed generally sympathetic and
said they would ask Noda for his opinion. Noda argued per-
suasively on my behalf, and I was given permission to go with
the delegation to Tokyo. Determined not to let such an oppor-
tunity slip by, I went to see Minowa Atsushi and Mizushima
Jun, two Aizu men who worked at the prefectural office, and
asked them to act as my guarantors. Minowa picked up his
brush without a moment's hesitation. He then composed a doc-

ument, gave it to Mizushima to add his name, and handed the paper to me. I submitted it immediately and obtained a firm promise from the officials.

Several days before we were scheduled to leave, I paid a visit to Noda to thank him for his many kindnesses. I owed him an immense debt, and knowing I would miss him, I wept. He gave me the money I had saved out of my wages—nine yen fifty sen, together with the money I had brought from Tanabu. The coins and paper notes, both old and new, came to about ten yen and eighty sen.[10] To this, he added three yen as a parting gift. I set aside one yen to spend on the trip, wrapped up the rest, and asked Nagaoka to keep it for me.

The people at the office congratulated me on my good fortune, and as a farewell present gave me an old red flannel undershirt, a secondhand Western-style umbrella, a cotton hand towel, and a *furoshiki*.* One of the men also lent me his derby hat on the condition that I wear it only as far as Tokyo. The hat, which was meant for an adult, was much too large and came down over my ears. When the owner subsequently came to Tokyo, I returned it to him with thanks.

The night before our departure, I went to thank Noda again. As I was about to leave, his mistress, Osono, her personal maid, Suzuki Mitsu, who was the daughter of an Aizu samurai, and the kitchen maid insisted on seeing me to the inn, where the officials were staying. Along the way, they gave me kind words of advice, and when I bowed to say good-bye, tears sprang to my eyes.

It was now the beginning of the sixth month. I strapped the bamboo traveling case to my back, tied on my straw sandals, and pulled the hat over my ears. Nagaoka rode on an ox-drawn cart while the rest of the delegation traveled on foot. He was a good-hearted man, and feeling sorry for me, he occasionally let me sit beside him or ride on one of the packhorses. At most, I walked ten or eleven miles a day.

*A *furoshiki* is a square cloth used to wrap and carry things.

We stopped the second day at Noheji—a place steeped in memories. I visited the Hinata family and told them I would be living in Tokyo. The following day, we stopped at Gonohe, where my uncle Kōzuki Kagetaka lived. At about this time, I learned that my father had finally despaired of farming in Oto-shinosawa and had moved to Shirihiki Village with Taichirō, who was temporarily out on bail.

At Sannohe, our next stop, I reported to the prefectural branch office that handled the affairs of the former domain. There I filled out the forms required to go to Tokyo. We stayed overnight at Fukuoka and left for Morioka.

Our stay in Morioka lasted a little more than a month. We were housed in a big mansion in Bakurō-chō that was owned by a man named Saitō. He was particularly nice to me and brought out a Western-style pitcher and glass tumbler for my amusement. He also gave me my first sip of beer; it was bitter and tasted like medicine. Saitō was the proud owner of the only rickshaw in Morioka and one evening treated me to a tour of the city.

My only responsibility during the trip was to accompany Nagaoka and Doi to the prefectural office in the morning and back to their lodgings in the late afternoon. I did this with another attendant, and as we took turns with a third attendant, I had little to do. I persuaded my fellow attendants to teach me arithmetic and reading.

The men completed their business in the middle of the seventh month. We headed for Toyoma, in Miyagi Prefecture, passing through Kurosawajiri, Mizusawa, and Ichinoseki. The work in Toyama finished, we boarded a boat and went down the Kitakamigawa River to Ishinomaki. From there, traveling close to the coastline, we continued southward to Matsushima. We stayed overnight, visited Shiogama Shrine by boat, and proceeded to Sendai.

We were scheduled to stay in Sendai for two days. I remembered that this was the hometown of Kurosawa Kamenoshin, alias Miyagi Shūtarō, the Chinese classics scholar whom Taichi-

rō had befriended in Tokyo and taken along to Tonami. He was in excellent health, and in his delight at seeing me, gave me a one-yen note.

The trip to Fukushima, our next destination, took two days. We stayed in the city for ten days; as before, I did no work apart from accompanying my superiors to and from the prefectural office. Morning glories, cockscombs, and Chinese asters were in full bloom—a reminder that we were now into autumn.

One morning, after I returned from the office, one of the attendants came up and gleefully thrust a paper packet under my nose. Inside were some lice he had found on my old flannel shirt. I snatched the shirt from him in a fury, tore it to shreds, and threw it away. I regretted this later, as the nights had turned decidedly colder. The attendant saw me shivering in misery and taunted me, saying I had no one to blame but myself.

We were now on the last leg of our trip. Traveling through Nihonmatsu, Motomiya, Miharu, and Ononiimachi, we arrived at Iwakitaira, our final destination. The work at the prefectural office took about ten days, and with all the business concluded, everyone was told they were free to do as they pleased. The two other attendants and I decided to go ahead to Tokyo. Before leaving, Ichikawa handed me a letter to take to his home in Tokyo; inside were instructions to let me stay at his home until his return.

We reached the outskirts of Tokyo on the morning of the twenty-first of the eighth month. As we walked on the main street in Senju, we noticed a fleet of rickshaws coming in our direction. I peered into one of them—and who should it be but Noda Hiromichi! I could hardly believe my eyes, much less utter a word. Noda saw me, stopped his rickshaw, and stared into my face. He recognized me as soon as I took off my derby hat. He was happy about our chance meeting and gave me his Tokyo address. He told me to come and see him in the near future.

I had at long last come to Tokyo, though as a lowly attendant with no knowledge of the complexities of politics. But I

was not alone in abandoning Tonami; shorn of any sense of purpose since the precipitate departure of the daimyo, several officials had secretly fled, "breaking off like the teeth of an old comb." My poor father and Sumi were unable to leave, however; as long as Taichirō remained under sentence, they would have to struggle on in Tonami and live in near starvation. I felt extremely bad about this.

Among those who had come to Tokyo was Yamakawa Ōkura. In Tonami, he had been determined to revive the fortunes of the daimyo house and surmounted all manner of obstacles to encourage production. He had succeeded in making farming tools with local iron sand and next looked into the possibilities of canning *hiragai* clams. To this end, he built up the port of Kominato. The project was well under way, but events had conspired against him. The abolition of the domains left him without a base of action, and especially with the daimyo gone, he saw no reason to remain. He made up his mind to leave the wilderness once and for all and seek a future in Tokyo. Noda, too, though not from Tonami, had been affected by the personnel changes brought about by the new prefectural system, and not long after my departure, he resigned from his position as vice-governor and came to Tokyo to start afresh. And, as I soon learned, he, like Yamakawa, was without employment. In the new world that had come into being, no one could be considered a full man unless he was a samurai from Satsuma, Chōshū, Tosa, or Hizen. The *bakufu* had been abolished, only to be replaced by a government monopolized by domain cliques. In this regard, perhaps I was fortunate to be a child. Unlettered and slow of wit, I could plead ignorance, grasp at any lead that came my way, and beg for help at every turn.

In any case, Ichikawa Masayasu had arranged for me to stay at his home in Shitaya Neribei-chō. After eating breakfast in the neighborhood, I went with my traveling companions to his house. A young man called Morikawa was in charge. He read the letter from Ichikawa, and together with the other live-

in students, promptly invited me in. After this, my companions headed for the Ōmura domain residence in Azabu, where they were expected.

During the trip, all my traveling expenses and incidentals had been paid by Nagaoka and Ichikawa. I was also given straw sandals, a hand towel, and sundry personal effects; the pocket money I carried had been more than sufficient to cover my needs.

In Tokyo, I hoped to see my brother Shirō. He had stayed on to study, but I now learned that he had recently left for Hachinohe to work at Hirosawa Yasutō's dairy farm as an interpreter for two foreign technicians.* I have already mentioned that Aizu was initially given the choice of relocating to either Inawashiro or Mutsu and that domain leaders had been inclined toward the latter, because Inawashiro was not only part of the old domain but much too small to sustain the samurai population. Furthermore, since the defeat the local economy and general morale had seriously deteriorated. In fact [in the tenth month of 1868], hundreds of peasants had risen in rebellion and called for fundamental changes—a "renewal of the world," as it was then called. Their authority at a low point, the domain leaders had lost all confidence in their ability to govern the area.[11] At this juncture, Hirosawa, who had just returned from a trip to Ezo [Hokkaido], had spoken up in favor of Mutsu. He claimed to have traveled through the Shimokita Peninsula and said he could vouch for its potential for development. The leaders had bowed to his opinion and had decided to settle in the far north. Then, after the abolition of domains and the departure of the daimyo and his senior officials, Hirosawa had chosen to remain in Tonami and operate a dairy farm. He invited two foreign experts, and in need of an interpreter, he hired Shirō. I was disappointed not to have my brother near me, but I knew he would benefit from the experience and quickly resigned myself.

*Shirō studied English with Numa Morikazu (1843–1890), a former *bakufu* retainer who studied with James Curtis Hepburn, the noted American missionary, in Yokohama.

Tokyo: The Old and the New

I had left Tokyo barely two years before [1870], but in my absence the city had been transformed into an imperial capital worthy of its new name. Even the people on the streets seemed to walk with a different step.

As a child, I had been unaware of the world beyond Aizu. My studies had been interrupted by the war, and after the defeat, I had been obliged to earn a living as a menial. In Tonami, too, I had put all my energies into surviving from one day to the next. At one point, I secretly planned to escape abroad, but when that failed, I had made up my mind to go to Tokyo, prepared to throw myself on the mercy of anyone willing to lend an ear. My efforts, I admit, did not spring from a lofty aspiration to "reach to the blue heavens" but from a desperate desire to escape from my situation.

When I first set foot in Tokyo, I had been a prisoner of war. My fellow captives and I had been herded into the city like a gang of beggars rounded up by the police. We had been put in a detention camp and spent each day in a state of humiliation. This time I was just as shabby, but at least I was not a captive. I wore a cotton kimono and *hakama*, a hat that came down over my ears, a pair of coarse straw sandals, and carried a bamboo traveling case on my back. I must have looked ludicrous, not that I or anyone else cared. In demeanor I was meek and humble and may even have struck others as obsequious. But

this was by no means intentional; I had always been timid, and my years of service as a menial certainly had not helped. I tried to change my ways, but it was no easy task, as that kind of temperament had long since become my second nature.

I also noted this time that many of the samurai had cut off their topknots and discarded their pair of swords. A number had even given up their *hakama*, preferring to wear their kimono loose, with a narrow sash tied round the waist. The previous year, in the eighth month, the government had announced that it would have no objections if samurai wanted to abandon their topknots and swords. But old customs die hard, and it was only human to see what others did before taking the final step. I myself had let my hair grow after Uncle Seisuke cut off my topknot to disguise me as a peasant boy. But cutting off one's topknot was apparently not so simple. Some asked their professional hairdressers, but found they were just as much in the dark. Others, fearful of being punished for doing something wrong, inquired at government offices. A set of instructions had consequently been issued:

> People may choose from the following. One: They may stop shaving their hair in front and pull the rest of the hair to the back (*sōhatsu*). Two: They may shave off their hair entirely (*teihatsu*). Three: They may cut off their topknots and let the hair grow long in the front and short in the back (*tekihatsu* or *zangiri*). Four: In contrast to the third choice, they may grow their hair short in front (*nadetsuke*) and even shorter in the back.

If cutting off one's topknot caused such confusion, what would happen in the future? Yesterday's authorities had been brought low and trampled under; lesser men sat in positions of power and lived in luxury. Shinto and Buddhism, united through the ages, had been forcibly separated by government decree; temples had been destroyed; entire castles had been razed. Ancestors were no longer properly venerated. What, indeed, was one to believe in? In a world marked by such disarray, my appearance was perhaps not all that strange. At any

rate, I had come to Tokyo without a clearly defined plan or specific base of action. Driven solely by a desire to reach this destination, I had done everything within my power to achieve this goal and had even lied about having relatives in the city.

There was one relative, however, who might help me—Kōsaka Osamu, the brother-in-law of my uncle Kōzuki Morizō. I had never met the man, but knew he worked at the Bureau of Shinto Affairs at the Education Ministry. I went to his office, but he said that he was busy all day and asked me to go to his house in Yotsuya in the evening.

I set off from Ichikawa's house in Shitaya and sought directions on the unfamiliar streets. I somehow took the wrong street, and after wandering through Sujichigaimon, Kandabashi, Wadakuramon, Sakuradamon, and Toranomon, I finally arrived at Kōsaka's house in Yotsuya Morisaka. But when I asked if I could stay with him, he refused point blank.

With no one else to turn to, I decided to visit him again a few days later. I walked as far as Sakuradamon and asked a passerby for directions to Yotsuya. He told me to go straight to Akasaka Mitsuke—Toranomon was out of the way—and to get further directions there. A ferry boat at Hasuike (later Tameike, Sannōshita) would take me there. At the crossing, however, I was told that a single fare cost one *mon*. Unwilling to spend even a penny, I continued walking.

As I passed in front of the main gate of the Hie Shrine, I noticed that a young beggar boy had thrust a bamboo pole through the slats in the wooden fence around one of the Niō statues. At the tip of the pole, he had rubbed bird lime, and this enabled him to pick up the coins the faithful had thrown inside. I thought I would imitate him and waited for him to leave. But suddenly, out of nowhere, I heard my mother whisper into my ear. Stabbed with remorse, I ran away as fast as I could.

At Kōsaka's house, I pleaded with him to reconsider. He lost his temper. "Haven't I already said no? What do you mean, coming here—don't ever show your face again!" He chased me out as if I were a beggar boy and then disappeared into his room.

All hope gone, I returned to Ichikawa's house. Everyone had finished supper, and though hungry, I went to bed wondering what I should do. No matter what, I knew I could not impose on Ichikawa much longer. I then remembered what Noda Hiromichi had said when we happened to meet the first day of my arrival in Tokyo. The next day I mustered my courage and went to his lodgings in Himono-chō. He said he was terribly sorry, but he was still unemployed and could not possibly help me. I was reluctant to drop the matter, for I had absolutely nowhere to go. In search of advice, I told him with complete candor about what I had done since leaving Aomori. He listened attentively, making no attempt to reproach me for the lie about having relatives in Tokyo, and urged me to return to Aomori or Tonami; he would call for me if anything turned up. I said I would rather die than go back, that I would bide my time, and come again to seek his advice. On the way back to Shitaya, I stopped at the home of Nasu Hitoshi, the finance ministry official who had once said he would help me, but he, too, curtly refused.

Then, Nagaoka Shigehiro, the official I had accompanied from Aomori, heard of my plight and offered to take me in for a while. I gratefully accepted and toward the end of the ninth month, moved into his house in Azabu Ichibei-chō.

Earlier in the same month, on the twelfth, the country's first railway line had opened between Tokyo and Yokohama. I went to Shinbashi Station for the event and took my seat on the bleachers. The train had just pulled in from Yokohama, and in a few minutes, the emperor alighted from his carriage. His Majesty was attired in persimmon-colored court robes and was accompanied by an entourage of officials, also in full court dress. Adding further to the splendor of the occasion was a host of foreign diplomats.

After the ceremony, I followed the crowd to the gardens of the Hama Detached Palace, which had been opened to the public for the day. A variety of entertainments was in progress. I caught sight of a man scattering red and white rice cakes on the

ground and hurried over to help myself.* It was already quite cold—the lunar ninth month would be the middle of October— but I wore only my cotton kimono and *hakama*. My crested *haori* and sword had been put away in the bamboo case until they were required.

I was still living in Nagaoka's house when I heard that Ōnuma Koshirō, an Aizu man, was teaching at a school in Hatchōbori Kameshima-chō. From Azabu Ichibei-chō it was some distance, but I was eager to attend his lectures on arithmetic and ran all the way. Then, between classes, I squatted down on the bare floor of the entrance and plied the teacher with questions to make up for my lack of knowledge. I also commuted to Shiba Akabane for reading lessons with Shimodaira Eiji, Yanagida Tomeroku, and Ōnuma Shironosuke— all Aizu men who were sharing lodgings. In both instances, I paid no tuition. With little time for study, however, I made scant improvement and began having doubts about my future.

At the end of the month, I received from Noda a letter of introduction he had written on my behalf to Nagaoka Hisashige and Yamakawa Ōkura.[12] I was deeply touched, for most of the men I knew were too busy seeking office and securing a toehold on the ladder of success to care what happened to a lowly attendant. Since arriving in Tokyo I had drifted from house to house and had yet to settle down; it was as if I had left the wilderness of Tonami only to wander in the wilderness of human affairs. But Noda had remembered me, and once again, I was filled with admiration for his selfless character. With this letter in hand, I went to Nagaoka Hisashige's house in Asakusa Kikuyabashi-dōri. He said he wished he could help me, but his small house was overflowing with his family and live-in students. He suggested that I go and talk to Yamakawa.

I headed straight for the Kanzō-in Temple in Asakusa Nagasumi-chō, where Yamakawa, former Aizu elder and vice-

*It is traditional to distribute red and white cakes on festive occasions, the combination of colors being considered auspicious.

governor of Tonami, had rented rooms. But I could tell at a glance that he was living under straitened conditions. Besides his own family, he was taking care of several students who were formerly from Aizu. He welcomed me, nevertheless, and said I could come any time. The household included his mother, his older sister Tokiwa, and two relatives, Kajiwara Kagekiyo and Nagai Kotarō. In addition, Yamakawa Tokuji, my nephew Kimura Ushitoku, Shimodaira Eiji, Yanagida Tomeroku, and other students seemed to come and go, staying overnight by turns. My presence would strain their circumstances further, but what was I to do?

Losing no time, I went to Ichikawa Masayasu's home in Shitaya to tell him the good news. His wife and his father, Masaya, in the meanwhile had come from Matsumoto to join him, and he had settled into a regular family life. He was pleased to hear I would be staying with Yamakawa, and his wife, noticing my light kimono and *hakama*, gave me a thick muslin undergarment with short sleeves. I put it on and took my leave, but as I walked along Shamisenbori-dōri, I began to perspire. I finally had to take it off and carry it on my arm. It was by then the tenth month, or November by the solar reckoning; wearing light clothes in the extreme winters of Shimokita had probably inured me to the cold.

I moved into Yamakawa's house sometime in the beginning of the tenth month. I was still wearing my soiled summer kimono. His mother and sister took pity on me and looked through the clothes his younger sister Sutematsu had left behind when she went to the United States to study.[13] They chose a pale purple cotton kimono with a design at the hem and a lining of peach-colored cambric; the sleeves had to be shortened, but otherwise it fit perfectly. I now went around dressed like a young girl and no doubt looked rather odd, but I did not mind as long as I was warm.

In the middle of the same month, Noda sent word that he wished to see me. He had probably heard about Yamakawa's finances and had found a job for me as a servant at the Tokyo residence of Yasuba Yasukazu, governor of Fukushima and fel-

low Kumamoto man. He said I would be living with Yasuba's mother, his wife, and two daughters. (The older daughter later became Baroness Yasuba, and the younger daughter, Gotō Shinpei's second wife.) Several students and a rickshaw puller also lived in the house. The family, he added, held to standards of correct behavior as befit their high social status.

At our first meeting, Mrs. Yasuba took one look at me and ordered a boy's *haori* of blue and white cotton. I wore this over my purple kimono; together with my *hakama*, they made a splendid outfit.

Soon after, on a wintry day, I visited Ichikawa to tell him that I had moved to the Yasuba residence. He saw my girl's kimono and asked his wife if there was something more suitable for a boy—something warm with cotton padding. The kind woman brought out a padded kimono that had belonged to Ichikawa's younger brother Masamori; it was made of black cotton and had the family crest dyed on the back. She adjusted the length for me, and with this, my winter wardrobe as a boy was complete.

At the Yasuba residence, I cleaned the house and garden once in the morning and again in the evening. I also served all the meals sitting near one end of the table. Apart from this, I accompanied the two daughters to their school in Kijibashi (probably the first girl's high school in Tokyo). I ran behind their rickshaw, carrying their book bags and lacquer lunch boxes, and when school was over, followed them in the same manner. One daughter was my age and the other a year younger, and while such duties were expected of a servant, they kept glancing back at me in commiseration.

Both Yasuba's mother and wife had a reputation for being exceptionally intelligent and capable. In speech and manner the family was very much in the samurai tradition. An ancestor, they were proud to note, had administered the final coup to the Akō samurai Ōishi Yoshio.* Had they known of my

*Ōishi Yoshio was the leader of the famous incident in which forty-seven samurai avenged the death of their lord, the daimyo of Akō, in 1702. Though widely admired for their loyalty, the participants were ordered by the *bakufu* to commit suicide.

antecedents, I am certain they would have treated me with more sympathy. As it was, I worked without pay—not even a copper penny—and received what personal effects I needed from the older students in the house.

The Happiest
Day of My Life

I had been working at the Yasuba residence for less than a month when Noda, who had recently been appointed a colonel in the Army Accounting Office, came to see me. He said, "Examinations will be held shortly to recruit students for the Army Cadet School.[14] Why don't you try taking them? If you pass, you can become a military officer. As the son of a samurai, you should have no objection."

Thunderstruck and wildly excited, I asked him then and there to act as my guarantor. I needed a second guarantor, so I talked to my benefactor Yamakawa Ōkura and sent in my application. I now had to cram for the examinations, and asked Miyagawa, one of the students at the Yasuba residence, to teach me reading and arithmetic.

Ever since the fall of Aizu, I had gone from job to job working as a servant and office attendant. Determined to earn my own living, I had struggled for months and days. I remember I was still living at Nagaoka's house when I heard that a printing shop in the neighborhood was looking for typesetters. I immediately applied, but was rejected on the ground that I did not know enough Chinese characters. Again, hearing that the Army Remount Bureau near the Hitotsubashi Gate was hiring farriers, I had gone to inquire about the application procedure but had been told I was underage. Now, as a servant at the Yasuba

residence, I felt hopelessly trapped until the moment Noda came to tell me about the school.

Early in the eleventh month, I went to the Bureau of Military Education just outside the Wadakuramon Gate to take the examinations. Among those taking the examination was Saitō Makoto, another of Noda's many protégés. (Saitō later became admiral, prime minister, and governor-general of the colonial government in Korea.) We were asked to read a passage each from the *Nihon gaishi* and *Nihon seiki** and to perform some simple arithmetic calculations. For composition, we had to write a letter to a friend in our hometown explaining why we wished to pursue a military career. A few oral questions and a physical examination followed. The results, we were told, would be announced early in the forthcoming year.

Noda dropped by at the end of the month to ask about the examinations. After I had given him the details, he nodded and said, "Well, that sounds about right." His words sent my heart soaring. When I thought about it later, I wondered if he had not already heard the results.

One evening, while on an errand near the Sujichigaimon Gate, I ran into Arakawa Tamezō, a student at Yamakawa's house. He said that Taichirō had been released on bail and had joined my father in Tanabu, but had subsequently returned to Tokyo under guard and was presently under house arrest at my cousin Suwa Takenosuke's home. He also said that the policeman who escorted my brother lived nearby and gave me his address. I went directly to the policeman's house. The policeman, who was from Aizu, explained that the case was now under the jurisdiction of the Justice Ministry, and that he had only been acting under orders to bring Taichirō to Tokyo. He assured me that Taichirō was in good health.

The next day, I explained the situation to Mrs. Yasuba and obtained permission to go to my cousin's house in Ueno Nezu Ikenohata. I had not seen my brother for two years. Overcome with both joy and sadness, I clung to him and wept. My

*These are histories of Japan written by Rai San'yō (1780–1832).

cousin's house, a so-called nine-by-twelve, was in a narrow alley, at the far end of a row of tenement houses. He lived with his [second] wife and a brood of children, making ends meet by cutting dried tobacco leaves. I did not see how the family could squeeze in another person, yet they had taken in my brother with utmost kindness. (The following year, my brother was put in a prison at the Justice Ministry.)

The government in the meantime had adopted the Western solar calendar and designated the third day of the twelfth month of Meiji 5 as January 1, 1873. This meant that New Year's Day came a month early, and at the Yasuba home, the family rushed about purchasing year-end gifts and preparing for the festivities ahead. But then, just three days before New Year's, word came that Governor Yasuba had been pitched from his horse and seriously injured. The family was thrown into turmoil and decided to move to Fukushima as soon as possible. They packed night and day and took off on the twenty-sixth, leaving word with Miyagawa to put the house in order and close it down within the year. No mention was made about my future.

I was told by Miyagawa to vacate the premises by the thirtieth, at the latest. I had been with the family for barely a month. I had nowhere to go, but orders were orders. I asked for a day's extension, and on the morning of New Year's Day, I packed my belongings and strapped the bamboo case to my back. As I was leaving, Miyagawa handed me a ten-sen note. His brother was governor of Nagasaki, and so he, unlike me, presumably had a place to go.

I walked aimlessly from Ogawamachi toward Nishiki-chō. Near an intersection, I spied a seedy-looking eatery that specialized in sweet *azuki*-bean soup. I went in and ordered two bowls—my New Year's breakfast, such as it was.* I paid six sen and ran out.

I continued walking as I wondered what to do and came to

*The *azuki*-bean soup presumably had rice cakes, which are traditionally eaten on New Year's Day with one's family.

the conclusion that I had no choice but to impose on Yamakawa yet again. With the remaining four sen, I bought a handful of kumquats and a packet of tissue paper to take as a gift and headed for his lodgings at the Kanzō-in, in Asakusa. Yamakawa was out, so I talked to his mother and sister and asked if I could stay until I heard from the Army Cadet School. The two women felt sorry for me, and without waiting for Yamakawa to return, invited me to stay.

Among the students living with the family was a relative, Nagai Kotarō, who was two years my senior. Together we read all the books we could put our hands on and studied arithmetic, asking the other students for help. I was treated like a member of the family, and other than occasional errands, had a great deal of spare time.

The family was in obvious financial distress. One of my errands was to take goods to a pawnshop in Asakusa Torigoe, and I did this more than two or three times a month. The meals were meager—an unvarying diet of tofu and boiled beans for everyone, including Yamakawa's mother. Another errand was to buy sweetened black beans—so-called *zazen mame*—at a neighborhood shop. I purchased three or four sen's worth at most, and brought it home wrapped in a bamboo sheath.

One day, Yamakawa and his mother said they wished to see me in private. "We hesitate to ask you this," he began, "but we are really at the end of our tether. Could we possibly borrow the money we've been keeping for you?" If Yamakawa, a former domain elder, had to ask me, who was actually just a servant, then he truly must have been in need. I agreed at once, of course, and he and his mother thanked me profusely. They looked greatly relieved. But to be frank, I was embarrassed and at a loss as to how to respond properly. The money in question was thirteen yen and fifty sen—the precious life savings I had guarded like the proverbial "lioness protecting her cub."

Over the following weeks, I stopped by the Bureau of Military Education to inquire whether I had passed the examinations. February came and went, and still I had not heard. Finally, on the very last day of March, came the good news: I had

been accepted! I was to report to school in Western dress. This was surely what was meant by dancing for joy; I felt as though I were floating on a cloud. Even my voice sounded a pitch higher, and yet, as I trembled with excitement, I could feel beads of perspiration breaking out on my forehead. I regretted to hear that Saitō Makoto had failed the examinations, but he was admitted to the Naval Academy the next year.

Yamakawa was every bit as delighted, and we took some of the money I had lent him and scoured the shops in Shiba Hikage-chō and Yanagihara for suitable clothes. We found a pair of gray, French-style trousers, a navy blue tunic with yellow braid and tassels, a French-style military cap, a pair of shoes, and undergarments. The purchases came to six or seven yen. Back at home, Yamakawa showed me how to wear the clothes, telling me to face this way and that, while the rest of the family looked on in approval.

The first day of school was April 1. The third was a national holiday commemorating the death of Emperor Jinmu. I went to visit the Yamakawa family and greeted them with the Western-style salute I had just learned. Everyone congratulated me and wished me the best for the future. Yamakawa's mother seemed particularly pleased. She put her hands on my shoulders and turned me around to get a better look. She had tears in her eyes, thinking, I am sure, of my mother and grandmother. In my happiness, I myself had not given them a thought, nor of my father still struggling in Tonami. This was inexcusable.

On the way back to school, I called on Noda Hiromichi. He surveyed me in my military uniform and broke into a smile. "Well, well, this ought to do, this ought to do." He kept repeating this in his native Kumamoto dialect, as if relieved to see that his past efforts had borne fruit. He seemed to take personal pride in my good fortune, even forgetting to give me the customary words of advice, and I, on my part, completely forgot to thank him.

I was indebted to Noda in more ways than I could count. [Like many other leaders in the government], he had studied with Yokoi Shōnan, but being from Kumamoto, he had been

excluded from the inner circles of government and prevented from attaining high office. In spite of this, he looked after young boys with complete impartiality and with no regard for which domain they came from; his only aim was the fostering of talent to build a new nation-state. And throughout, instead of lecturing or sermonizing, he treated everyone with kindness and patience.

My next visit was to my other benefactors, Nagaoka and Ichikawa. I greeted them, too, standing at attention with a smart salute. As I dashed from house to house, the hem of my blue tunic flapped in the April breeze. It was then the height of the cherry blossom season, and the people thronging the streets stopped and stared at me, while whispering to one another. I was as proud as a peacock, my heart brimming with joy. Though I had nothing particular to do, I roamed the city streets until dark. Truly, that was the happiest day of my life.

Military School

There were ten or so new students at the school. Of these, Ishimoto Shinroku (later lieutenant general, army minister, and baron) and Ishii Hayata (later lieutenant general) were older students who had transferred from the Daigaku Nankō (now Tokyo University) and already knew some French. The other students included Mabuchi Masabumi (later major general), Yamaguchi Masaru (later lieutenant general), and Nagamine Genkichi (later colonel). Yamaguchi, at twelve, was the youngest. I was fifteen, and the rest were either fifteen or sixteen.

The school was under the jurisdiction of the Army Bureau of Military Education. Lieutenant Colonel Kawakatsu Hiromichi served as principal, and the vice-principal was a civilian named Nakao Sutekichi. The teachers were all French: the head instructor Pouset, as well as Moncet, Vencien, Lechet, Goupele, and Louis.* The Japanese on the staff acted merely as interpreters. Subjects such as Japanese literature and history, moral education, and calligraphy were not offered. Instruction was exclusively in French. We even recited the multiplication table in French, and in geography and history classes, we studied about France. Once in a while, we would learn something about Japanese geography or history, but mainly we memorized facts about France—its mountains and rivers, cities and vil-

*The spelling is taken from Shiba's manuscript.

lages, climate, and so on, which we would then be called on to recite.* We knew nothing of the instructors' background; I imagine that they were hired from among the foreign residents in Yokohama and Kobe. Years later, when stationed in Paris as a captain or major, I happened to hear that Pouset was the proprietor of a small café. But my better judgment told me not to look him up.

I was placed in the lowest class, with Yamaguchi and several other new students. We began with our ABCs, practicing pronunciation, but we also had to attend the same lectures as the students who had entered a year ahead. Needless to say, I was unable to make head or tail of what was being said; at this rate, I felt I would never catch up, no matter how much I studied. I nonetheless threw myself into my studies and worked straight through the holidays, often awash in tears of frustration. Swaggering down the streets in my navy blue uniform was out of the question.

To begin with, as an Aizu native, I was unable to distinguish the sounds denoted by *i* and *e*, *ri* and *yu*. I was ridiculed by my classmates for this, but worse, it meant I would never be able to master even the rudiments of the French language. My grades were shameful, and sad to say, I was invariably at the bottom of the class.

The meals at the school were also Western—soup, bread, meat. On Saturdays, just for a change, we would be given rice with curried meat for lunch. Unaccustomed to the diet, most students complained about the food, but for me, life at school—with the exception of my French studies—was like heaven on earth.

All this time, Taichirō had been awaiting trial. The judicial and administrative branches of the government had undergone frequent changes, and as a result, my brother could be released on bail one day only to be arrested again and sent back to jail the

*The French influence at the school reflects the *bakufu*'s earlier reliance on French military instructors.

next. The months had lengthened into years, with no prospect of the case ever being resolved. For the present, he was out on bail but forbidden to leave Tokyo; he had been obliged to go from house to house, living off relatives, friends, and acquaintances. At school, we were given ten sen for spending money on holidays, so after first paying the laundry bill, I bought some fruit—a favorite of his—and went to see Taichirō whenever I could.

The whole affair was disheartening. My brother's only offense had been taking responsibility for a crime he had not committed. Thanks to him, famine had been averted and the domain was spared a huge financial loss. The men at the Justice Ministry, as well as the former daimyo and his officials, were fully cognizant of this, but as the plaintiff was a Danish national, they were reluctant to proceed with the litigation. Instead, they were content to make my brother a scapegoat. Moreover, not a single domain official had come forward to express a word of gratitude or consolation. One might suppose that the former daimyo, now a member of the new nobility, or his former officials—all capable men—would come to his rescue. They knew my brother had been unjustly imprisoned for three years, but they were intimidated by the new government and had refused to lift a finger. I was young and unacquainted with affairs of the world, but I was still saddened and angry. Was this what the samurai code had come to? And what had happened to the much-vaunted spirit of Aizu?

It was a new era, and life was pitiless. In a harsh world where each day brought dizzying changes, even the men of Aizu seemed to have forgotten the meaning of duty and honor. In the feudal past, when social status and office had been determined by birth, one at least knew the proper channels for seeking employment. But now, people were being thrown out on the streets and left to fend for themselves. True, they had been liberated from the fetters of feudalism and in a sense were free to choose, but thus far, no industries had been established, and as for government jobs, they were monopolized by men from Satsuma, Chōshū, Tosa, and Hizen. For people from Aizu, in

particular, Tokyo was yet another Tonami—a hostile waste-
land. With people worn down by the demands of daily life, per-
haps it was all too easy to forget the obligations of the past.

And I myself had changed. A cadet at a military school, I
wore a French uniform, dined on French food, and drilled
French-style. Every day, together with the other students, I
practiced at the Hibiya Parade Ground—now Hibiya Park but
then a grassy field stretching all the way from the palace moat.
"*Attention!*" "*En avant marche!*" I marched to the commands
of the French drill master. As if to herald a new age, the air
echoed with the sounds of a foreign tongue and of our boots
stamping the ground.

As summer drew near, the students' conversation turned to
holiday plans—going home, taking trips, finding lodgings in
Tokyo. I had nowhere to go, and once again, moved into
Noda's house at Surugadai to work as a servant.

Another student, named Takeuchi, also lived in the house.
He was from Kumamoto and six or seven years older than I.
Accustomed to working as a servant, I set aside my uniform
and promptly set to work. Rising early, I cleaned the house and
garden, sprinkled water outside to settle the dust, greeted Noda
when he woke up, rolled up the quilts and stored them in the
cupboards. I performed these duties as a matter of course, and
Noda, for his part, raised no objection. But Takeuchi, who took
all of this in, heartily disapproved. Several days after I had
moved in, he beckoned me to the students' room, near the front
entrance. With a stern look on his face, he said, "I don't know
a thing about your background, or the reasons for your behav-
ior. But I do know that you are a student at the Army Cadet
School, and that in the future you will be entrusted with the
defense of our country. So why are you demeaning yourself like
this, working like a common servant?

"First of all," he continued, "I've seen you putting away the
master's bedding. And if that isn't bad enough, I've seen you
putting away his mistress' soiled quilts. That kind of work is
meant for the lowliest of the low—it's too painful to watch. If
you continue like this, you'll never amount to anything. I shud-

der to think about what effect this will have on the Imperial Army. Take my advice and leave this place at once."

I thought the matter over. He was right, but it had nothing to do with Noda; his brazen mistress was to blame. I quickly put on my uniform, left the house, and made arrangements to move in with Arisaka Nariakira, an assistant to the French language instructor. (He later became lieutenant general and baron.) Taichirō, who was still under house arrest, came to thank Arisaka personally. The school had given us three yen and fifty sen as food money for the summer. I persuaded Arisaka to take the entire amount to help out with expenses. Arisaka's lodgings were in Kōjimachi Go-chōme, on the second floor of a store called the Kajimaya. In hopes of being better prepared for the fall term, I asked him to tutor me in French and other subjects.

Back at school, I found to my chagrin that I was unable to keep up with the lessons. I resolved to push myself harder, and after lights-out, hid in the lavatory and pored over my books. On some nights, I smuggled a small oil lamp out of the lavatory, waited until everyone was asleep, and studied huddled under a blanket. It is a wonder I did not start a fire or die from asphyxiation.

In April, Meiji 7 [1874], I was promoted to the second year. I was at the bottom of the class, seemingly condemned to stay there forever. I found this extremely galling. To console myself, I thought up all kinds of excuses—that I did not have the benefit of a formal education, that Satsuma and Chōshū were ultimately to blame, and so on. I was introverted by nature anyway and began to brood. I became despondent, even bitter. If things continued this way, I would have to withdraw. But I had made a promise to my father: "I shall not return until I have made something of myself." No matter what happened, I had to persevere. I reminded myself of the promise I had made in Tonami and studied with renewed fervor.

One day, in composition class, we were assigned to write on "A French Monarch Beloved by His Subjects for His Kindness and Mercy." Monsieur Vencien, our teacher, first went over the

story in detail. He then told us to write it in our own words and submit it on a certain date.

On the day the assignment was due, we were told to read our compositions out loud. We read in order of class ranking, but after two or three sentences, the teacher would shout "No good!" and make the student sit down. The twenty or so students who preceded me had all failed; it was now my turn. In fear and trembling, I started to read, but the teacher inexplicably kept nodding, interjecting a remark here and there about a mistake in phrasing. When I had finished, he said, "*Très bien!* This is the way a composition should be written." I could not believe my ears. Monsieur Vencien then corrected my composition in red ink and dictated it to the class. I was utterly mystified, as were all my classmates, who looked at me in wonderment.

"*Très bien!*" The teacher's words cast to the winds the sense of inferiority that had caused me such pain. No longer did I shed tears over my lessons or push aside my books in mortification. On the contrary, studying was now a positive pleasure, and once again, the future seemed bright with promise. My grades in Monsieur Louis' history class also improved. My work was held up as a model, my marks rose with each test, and most important, I was no longer at the bottom of the class.

A series of events had meanwhile unsettled the country. The previous year [in May] a huge fire had swept the Imperial Palace, and [in October] Saigō Takamori, whose proposal to invade Korea had been overruled, had resigned as government councilor and returned to Satsuma.* Then, earlier this year, a rebellion led by Etō Shinpei had broken out in Saga, in western Kyushu.† In

*Government leaders at the time were divided over the question of whether to send an expeditionary army to Korea. The proponents felt that Korea should be punished for refusing to recognize the restoration of imperial rule in Japan; they also were aware that an expedition would provide employment for indigent samurai. Opponents of the expedition felt that Japan was too weak and feared the international reaction.

†In February, 1874, Etō Shinpei (1834–1874), who also resigned over the so-called Korean Question, led several thousand former samurai who opposed the government's modernizing programs in a short-lived rebellion. He and eleven of his followers were executed.

fact, Yamakawa [who eventually found employment with the army and became a major] had left his home in Nezu to fight in Kyushu. More recently [in May] Japanese troops had invaded Taiwan [in retaliation for the massacre of Okinawan fishermen in 1871]. Negotiations with China were under way, but at this stage, a full-scale war could not be ruled out. I remember going to the Ginza with my classmates to see a young female aborigine who had been taken captive in Taiwan.

It was about this time that the school was honored with a visit from the emperor. His Majesty observed classes and drills and later most graciously conveyed a few words of encouragement to Soga [Sukenori], head of the Bureau of Military Education. Pouset, the head instructor, expressed his appreciation in French, and this was duly translated by Prince Fushimi Sadanaru, a student.

We dispersed for summer vacation in August. Taichirō, who was out on bail, had rented a room in a vacant house near Kandabashi Gate owned by someone called Honda. My brother Shirō was also in Tokyo, having left his job at the dairy farm. We decided to share lodgings; my summer food allowance of four yen would amply cover our expenses. To cook our meals, we bought a big iron pot to replace Taichirō's small, earthen pot, built a mound of rocks and tiles under the eaves, and on top placed an unglazed brazier, also newly purchased. With several days' supply of rice and miso, we were now ready.

Shirō was still sickly, so I took on the cooking. As I mentioned, he had always suffered from poor health and was alive only because he had been in bed with a fever at the time of the war. Other survivors of his company, the Byakkotai, included Yamakawa Ōkura's younger brother Kenjirō (later president of Tokyo Imperial University), Takamine Hideo (later principal of Tokyo Higher Normal School and Tokyo School of Fine Arts), Akabane Yashirō (later a student abroad and eventually a diplomat), Ibuka Kajinosuke (graduate of Tokyo Itchi Theological School and founder of Meiji Gakuin University), and Iinuma Sadakichi (army captain and later chief of the Sendai Postal Bureau), who attempted suicide at Iimoriyama but miraculous-

ly survived. Each and every one of them represented the best of Aizu.

I also hoped to nurse my brother back to health and went to the river behind the Kōbusho to dig for *shijimi* clams.* This was a place I remembered all too well from my days as a prisoner of war. I put the clams in miso soup, but someone from Nagaoka in Tosa saw me cooking one day and gave me a tip: If I put the clams into a pot of boiling water and threw in a handful of ashes, the clams would separate from the shells; then, to make *tsukudani* preserve, all I had to do was simmer them in soy sauce. I followed his advice and cooked up large batches for my brother. Also, for good measure, I boiled large amounts of beans and wrapped them in bamboo sheaths for his future use.

I bought a cotton kimono to wear for the summer, but as a new sash seemed an unnecessary expense, I made do with a strip of cloth torn from an old *furoshiki*.

The six weeks of vacation passed quickly, but I was reluctant to leave Shirō, for he had no one to look after him or fetch his medicine. Taichirō was away at work most of the day, though what he did, I was not sure. Undoubtedly, it had something to do with putting records in order at the old domain residence or helping out at a government office; his wages, I suspect, were minimal.

At school, my grades continued to improve; I was now in the upper half of my class. I had never been fond of games, debates, or any form of competition, nor did I frequent entertainment halls or restaurants. Instead, on school holidays, I went with friends of similar interests to visit old battlefields and the graves of famous men. We also combed the shops for portraits of Napoleon, Washington, Enomoto Takeaki, Ōtori Keisuke, and other great men and heroes we admired. Of course, I refused to touch a portrait of anyone from Chōshū or Satsuma.

One of my heroes, Enomoto Takeaki, had just returned

***Shijimi* (*Corbicura atrata*), a rich source of the amino acid taurine, was traditionally considered a cure-all, especially for jaundice.

from Russia.* I made up my mind to visit him. A reckless idea, to be sure, but I was completely earnest at the time. I went to his home in Kudanshita Imagawakōji but was turned away at the door. I returned to his house for three Sundays running and was refused each time. I persisted, however, and at last, his patience doubtless worn thin, Enomoto agreed to see me. He was much fiercer than I had imagined from his photograph.

"What do you want?" he demanded.

"Sir, I realize I am still young, but permit me to say that I have long admired you and think you are the greatest person alive in Japan. Would you have some advice for me?"

"First, build up your physical strength. Second, be honorable and fair. Third, acquire learning. That's all."

He stood up to leave the room. "In future, I'll see you if I'm free. Just identify yourself at the door as Shiba Gorō from the Army Cadet School."

Enomoto was extremely brusque, and perhaps because of my earlier experiences, I still took offense at the tiniest slight. I felt he had been barely able to tolerate me—an impudent brat—and never went back.

When I first entered the school, in Meiji 6, it had been run entirely on the French model, with its curriculum a replica of primary school education in France. Japanese literature, geography, or history had hardly been mentioned. All this changed in Meiji 8 [1875].

A visit by army inspectors had been scheduled. The buildings were given a thorough cleaning, and our uniforms were inspected and spruced up. An elaborate Western-style luncheon with many courses was prepared for the entire school. The inspectors, however, were horrified. Nothing was said that day, but their report was given serious consideration by the senior officers, and before long, the old heads were replaced by Captain Iwasaki Motonori, who became the new principal, and

*Enomoto Takeaki (1836–1908), the *bakufu* naval commander who held out in Hokkaido, was pardoned in 1872. He was sent to Russia in 1874 to negotiate the exchange of Sakhalin for the Kurile Islands.

Lieutenant Mizuyama Tadashi, who became vice-principal. Regulations were tightened, and the school was run more like an army camp. Disciplinary action, which at most had consisted of confinement to school grounds, now included incarceration in a lockup expressly built for this purpose. The last measure came as a shock to the students. They became extremely angry and complained loudly that as future officers and guardians of national defense, they were being gravely insulted.

The French-style curriculum was also modified to include such traditional texts as the *Nihon gaishi* and *Bunsho kihan*.* School records and other documents were written with brush and ink in Japanese instead of in French. The uniform of gray trousers, French-style cap, and blue tunic with yellow braid and tassels was discarded in favor of dark blue trousers with thin yellow stripes on the side and a black Dolman jacket with rows of braiding across the chest. This was eventually replaced by a German-style tunic with stand-up collar and red chevrons.†

The number of foreigners on the staff also dwindled, elementary French, for example, being taught by a Japanese. Such changes, of course, affected those of us who had entered under the old system. We were fluent in French and familiar with French history, geography, and customs, but knew precious little about our own country, and this included reading or writing classical Japanese or Chinese. In fact, for this very reason, several students had failed to advance to the Officers Academy. But such confusion and contradiction were not peculiar to military education in the formative years of the army. In public schools as well, translations of American textbooks were being used without any modification. Only when these were replaced by official Japanese textbooks could one say, perhaps, that the true work of the Restoration had begun.

Compared to me, Shirō was very well read. Confined to

*The *Bunsho kihan* (Ch. *Wenchang kueifan*) is a Sung dynasty collection of ancient writings used as a model for composition.

†The switch to German-style uniforms was a part of the army's adoption of the German military model in the aftermath of the Franco-Prussian War of 1871.

bed for long periods, he had studied on his own and become proficient in English. He would later go to the United States to study, and on his return, write *Chance Meetings with Beautiful Women* (Kajin no kigū), one of Japan's first political novels. He would also be elected to parliament and appointed parliamentary undersecretary. In short, his career would seem to confirm the proverb that "men of talent are prone to sickness."*

Taichirō's case was finally brought to court in late December of Meiji 9 [1876], nearly seven years after the Danish consul had first pressed charges. In view of the extenuating circumstances—my brother had taken sole responsibility for the affair and implicated no one else—he was given a sentence of one hundred days in prison. The existing legal system made no allowance for time spent as an unconvicted defendant, and so he was committed again to Ichigaya Prison.

Each Sunday, I took him personal necessities—food and other items that were permitted to prisoners. Because direct communication was forbidden, I wrote notes in tiny script on a scrap of thin rice paper and tucked it inside a packet of tooth powder. For news about my brother, I relied on verbal or written messages he entrusted to discharged prisoners.

I was also in touch with Gosaburō, who wrote at rare intervals. He, my father, and Sumi had given up farming in Tonami and returned to Aizu, where they would be close to the family grave. Shirō was in better health but still frail, and after working briefly in Yokohama, was back in Tokyo recuperating at his lodgings in Soto Kanda Matsuzumi-chō. All three brothers had been dogged by bad luck and would contend with misfortune for some time more.

In the government, high offices continued to be monopolized by former samurai from Satsuma, Chōshū, Tosa, and Hizen. The few outsiders who gained employment were usually relegated to some minor position and were at the beck and call of their superiors. At the same time, even as the work of the

*The full proverb is "Men of talent are prone to sickness and beautiful women destined to die young."

Restoration had yet to be completed, signs of rupture had begun to appear within the government clique. The growing disturbance in Kyushu was one instance.*

The Restoration meant different things to different domains: Some were bent on maintaining the status quo, others, on wresting political leadership, while the rest only wished for peace and quiet. Within the domains themselves, too, people disagreed, their ideals and objectives as different as the proverbial "mixture of gold and dross." A reaction against the government's attempts to force unanimity and conformity to its policies was, perhaps, inevitable.†

At school, where the students came from various domains, we were as a rule circumspect in expressing our opinions. We now especially avoided talk about the unrest in Kyushu, but as the subject was on everyone's mind, this seemed forced and unnatural.

Beginning in the summer of Meiji 9, the students who did not go home or find lodgings elsewhere had been given permission to live at school. I stayed on with about twenty students.

*When Saigō left for Satsuma (now Kagoshima Prefecture) in October 1873, he was accompanied by some six hundred soldiers and policemen who were originally from that domain. They subsequently dominated the prefectural government and openly criticized the central government's policies, in particular the gradual stripping of samurai privileges. Fearing a revolt, on January 30, 1877 the government sent a naval vessel to take possession of the weapons in the Kagoshima arsenal, but the government force was driven off by about one thousand Satsuma soldiers, who then took the weapons themselves. A rumor also circulated of a government-instigated plot to assassinate Saigō, who had played no part in the incident. Pushed by his followers, Saigō decided to march to Tokyo to demand an explanation for the harassment. In February, at the head of several thousand armed men, he advanced as far as Kumamoto Castle, the site of a government garrison. It was at this point that the "rebellion" began.

†This paragraph is another example of Ishimitsu's insertion of history with his own interpretation.

The Satsuma Rebellion

As I mentioned, the government had split in two over the question of sending an army to Korea. When Saigō Takamori, Itagaki Taisuke, and other advocates of war were defeated, they resigned from office. Saigō returned to his home base in Satsuma, followed by his confidant Kirino Toshiaki and hundreds of young men from the elite Konoe Guards. [They were now rumored to be plotting an insurrection], and the turmoil in political and military circles had reached the point where some were privately predicting a second restoration was at hand. To make matters worse, on October 20 [actually, October 24, 1876], the Jinpūren, a band of conservative former samurai from the Kumamoto domain, had risen in rebellion and forced their way into the local garrison. Within days, like-minded samurai revolted in Akizuki and Hagi.* At our school, the students from Satsuma had spent the summer living at the domain residence in Nagata-chō, but instead of returning to classes in September, had left for Kyushu to join Saigō and Kirino.

The new year [1877] dawned. On the fourth, the soldiers stationed at the Tokyo garrison were called out for emergency duty at the Imperial Palace gates. Military exercises were also held at the Hibiya Parade Ground to demonstrate to the public that the army was fully prepared to meet the crisis in Kyushu.

*All three revolts were immediately suppressed.

The same month, our school was formally merged with the Army Officers Academy and moved to new quarters on the academy campus in Ichigaya.

On February 18, amid rumors of an imminent insurrection in the Kagoshima area, the First Infantry Regiment of the Konoe Guards was ordered to Kyoto. A large contingent of army and navy officers and bureaucrats from the Home Ministry immediately followed. In my diary for February 20, I note the following entry: "I am not certain of the truth of the matter, but I hear that imperial orders have been issued to quash the potato samurai. What wonderful, wonderful news!"

Two days later, on the twenty-second, the principal made an announcement: "This is to inform you of a communiqué we received on the nineteenth from His Majesty's temporary residence in Kyoto. In light of conclusive evidence that armed elements from Kagoshima have forcibly entered Kumamoto Prefecture, imperial orders have been issued for their immediate suppression. Prince Arisugawa Taruhito will serve as supreme commander."

On March 3, ninety-six infantry specialists in the first entering class of the upper school were assigned as officer trainees to garrisons in Tokyo, Osaka, and Nagoya.* On the twentieth, students from the academy, including the lower school, and students from schools for noncommissioned officers were ordered to join soldiers stationed in Tokyo to take part in a large-scale maneuver. We assembled at the Hibiya Parade Ground and marched through the city streets to Etchūjima. Attending the exercises were all officers stationed in Tokyo, and ministers and other members of the foreign diplomatic corps.

At school, we could not help but be distracted by these events. In this regard, the principal had issued a warning four days earlier, on the sixteenth: "As you know, because of the

*Students at the academy were identified by the order in which they entered the school. Thus, the students who entered the school at its formal establishment as the Rikugun Shikan Gakkō in 1875 were known as the first entering class (*ikkisei*). Shiba, who entered in 1877, was a member of the third entering class.

conflict in southern Kyushu, the students in the first entering class specializing in infantry and other fields have been assigned to regimental duty. As the situation now stands, there will probably be no further call for a second contingent of students. I therefore urge you not to be swayed by idle rumors, but to make good use of your time and attend to your studies so that you have no reason for regret later."

We tried to stay calm and concentrate on our studies, but it was difficult, especially since we now heard a rumor that Kumamoto Castle, the site of the Kyushu garrison, had surrendered to Satsuma soldiers. On the twenty-seventh of March, I received a letter from Shirō: "This very day I am leaving Tokyo to fight with government forces in Kyushu. If I do not seize the chance to take revenge on Satsuma, I shall never be able to face those who rest in their graves in Aizu. Let us meet on the day of victory. Until then, work diligently at your studies." I was alarmed, for I knew that he was leaving his sickbed to go to the front, but as I myself was seething to fight the enemy, I made no move to stop him and prayed for his safe return in triumph.

Taichirō was nearing the end of his sentence and looking forward to his release from prison. I very much wanted to do something in the way of a celebration, but with Shirō away at the front, I was unsure how to proceed. I was also extremely busy. My Sundays and holidays were spent taking provisions to Taichirō, as well as trying to obtain information about Noda, who was in Kagoshima fighting, and Kimura Ushitoku, who was at Kumamoto Castle. Getting provisions to Taichirō was particularly time consuming. A stamped approval was required from the Ichigaya ward office, but as the office was closed on Sundays, I had to go to the home of the head officer Shibata Norikane to get special permission.

Taichirō was finally released on April 6—a free man for the first time since the move to Tonami. Reunited at long last, we shed tears of joy and relief. My brother said he would stay for the time being at Akabane Shirō's house in Surugadai.

On April 11, the students in the second entering class were commissioned as officer-trainees; half the students were

assigned to Kyushu, and the other half were sent as instructors to training schools for noncommissioned officers at various regiments in Tokyo. The students in the lower school who were judged of sufficient height were also issued firearms and trained in their use. This made us even more restless, and on free days, some of the students went to shooting galleries in town to practice their skills, or to the hills in Ueno to indulge in drink and song. Others visited the homes of the principals of both schools and begged to be sent to the front.

With all the upper-level students assigned to field service, the authorities decided to let the students in the lower school move up one year. Examinations, which were held for one day only, covered a wide range of subjects. We were asked to punctuate and give Japanese readings of passages from the *Nihon seiki* and *Hachidaika*,* write a composition in classical Japanese, translate from French, and do problems in fractions, algebra, and geometry. My luck was good, and I passed.

While I was taking the examinations, Taichirō apparently had come to see me. According to the staff member who spoke with him, his request to serve in Kagoshima had been granted, and he was leaving that same day. I was very sorry that I had missed him, but I could well imagine what he was thinking: Not only had he been released from prison but he was going to Kagoshima to assist in the postwar disposition of our sworn enemy. I also thought of my father in Aizu and of how deeply gratified he must be to see Satsuma humiliated after all these years. As I pictured him at the grave reporting the news to my grandmother, mother, and sisters, I clasped my hands in silent prayer.

My brother Gosaburō was just as determined not to stand idly by. He entrusted my father to Sumi's care and came all the way from Aizu. He was too late, however, and though he tried in every way possible to be sent to the front, he was unable to find a suitable position. He then heard that the Tokyo Metro-

*The *Hachidaika* (Ch. *Patachia*) is a collection of writings by eight T'ang and Sung dynasty writers compiled by the Ming scholar Mou K'un.

politan Police was seeking new recruits. The agency had decided to send volunteers from its own ranks to fight in the war, but because many in the force were from Aizu and only too glad to go, there had been a sudden shortage in personnel. Gosaburō leapt at the chance and promptly was made the head of a hundred-man unit.[15] I should also mention that before leaving, Taichirō had left one hundred yen with Gosaburō to send to my father.* Thus, by the most fortuitous of circumstances, all four brothers had gathered in Tokyo, each determined to wreak vengeance on Satsuma. I was exultant.

I also learned that Yamakawa Ōkura, who had changed his first name to Hiroshi, had been promoted to lieutenant colonel. He had landed with his troops in Yatsushiro in Kumamoto Prefecture, intercepted the retreating Satsuma soldiers, and cornered them at Hyūga Pass. (He later became major general and a member of the House of Peers.) Yamakawa, my brothers, and other men from the same province and domain who had suffered the same fate were together fighting to redeem the honor of Aizu. What could be more glorious! Words could not describe my tremendous joy.

I was formally admitted to the Officers Academy on May 4. I heard frequently from Taichirō and Shirō, who addressed their letters to Gosaburō, but in a while they began writing to me directly, no doubt assuming he had left for the front.

I received a letter from my father for the first time in my life. It was five years since I had last seen him in Tonami. I was certain he had written in a moment of jubilation and satisfaction. Though he made no mention of my brothers at the front, I rather imagined he had first gone with Sumi to pray at the family grave, and then come home and taken up his brush. I read the letter over and over, unable to check the tears.

*Soldiers going to the front received a bonus allowance, the amount depending on rank.

End of the Satsuma Rebellion

It was now October [1877]; the remnants of the Satsuma forces had been crushed, and Saigō had committed *seppuku*.* Taichirō was the first to return from Kyushu. As he was anxious to give a full report to my father, he hastened home to Aizu. Shirō returned, too, as promised, in triumph, but in such poor health he had to be hospitalized.

The members of the first entering class, all of whom had eventually gone to the front, returned some time after those of the second entering class. More than thirty in the class were dead. The surviving fifty or so students were commissioned either second lieutenants or probationary second lieutenants.

I was nearing the end of my second year and had to choose a special field.[†] Qualifying examinations were scheduled for December. After consulting with Shirō and Gosaburō, I decided to specialize in the artillery. I sat for examinations and passed. I then took the opportunity to get rid of the tapeworm that had plagued me for years, and entered the school infirmary for a starvation cure.

The night I entered the infirmary, a big melee broke out

*Kirino Toshiaki also died. It was he who accepted the surrender of the Aizu Castle in 1868.

†Students specializing in artillery or engineering spent an extra (third) year at the academy.

between the students in the second entering class and the third entering class—my class. Several students were hurt. The reason for the fight was simple enough: The older students had seen something of the world—some had even engaged in mortal combat—and were too overwrought to settle down. They tended to get drunk and treat the younger students with disdain. One of them had gotten out of hand again, and a classmate of mine, a brawny youth named Ogawa Hiroo, had become incensed and punched him. This set off a free-for-all. An excess of youthful exuberance, surely, but the school authorities refused to take it lightly. They regarded this as a breach of military discipline and brought the case before a court martial. Large numbers of students from both classes were forbidden to leave the grounds and underwent cross-examination. For better or for worse, I was not involved and could leave campus as usual. I paid several calls on the head judge, Colonel Kurokawa Michinori, and appealed to him for a swift and lenient disposition of this matter. The trial dragged on for nine months. In the end, the students were confined to school for three weeks.

In February [1878], Gosaburō resigned from the police force and returned to Aizu; he had never had a chance to fight the enemy. Gosaburō was to remain by my father's side almost continuously, a devoted son to the last, carrying the burden the brothers should have shared, unable to make his mark in the world.

Home Minister Ōkubo Toshimichi was assassinated in May.* Both he and Saigō came from low-ranking samurai families in Satsuma, and they had played together as children, since their families had been very close. But on the question of war against Korea, Saigō, who valued duty and loyalty to friends above all else, and Ōkubo, who was a realistic and rational politician, had come to a parting of the ways. Then, in the war last year, they had been the leaders of opposing armies. Now,

*Ōkubo was assassinated by a former samurai who felt that Saigō had been wronged.

within months of each other, they were both dead. The two men undeniably had become pillars of the nation, but to me, they were still arch-villains. At the time of the Restoration, they conspired and decided that [dramatic] military action was necessary, and following the saying that "the attention of the nation must be claimed in order to achieve great deeds," they had made Aizu their blood sacrifice. I could not bring myself to forgive them and did not feel an iota of sympathy. In my opinion, arrogance and recklessness had been their undoing; their violent deaths were the logical conclusion of their actions.

Such effusions are typical of naïve youth, and to this day, I am not ashamed of these emotions. On occasion, my fellow students would be carried away, too, and more than once went on strike protesting what they considered unreasonable demands or unfair grading by their instructors. Many of these students later became field marshals, generals, and lieutenant generals, and so I see no need to censure them for their youthful excesses.

It was the twenty-third of August and ten years to the day since my grandmother, mother, and sisters had died in the name of honor. [My cousin Suwa Takenosuke had also lost his wife during the siege], and in hopes that we might pray together in remembrance, I went to his house in Ushigome Tsukudo. I limped all the way, dragging my legs, which were swollen from beriberi. To my disappointment, my cousin was not at home nor were there any signs of preparation. I went back to my summer lodgings, offered my prayers in solitude, and sat in quiet recollection.

That same day, in the middle of the night, I was startled from sleep by the ringing of fire bells. I flung open the windows and saw flames raging in the direction of the Takehashi garrison. I also heard the steady boom of cannons, but since this was routine procedure whenever a fire broke out near the Imperial Palace, I decided to go and see it with Furuichi, another student lodger. We walked as far as Ōkuma Shigenobu's residence in Kijibashi-soto. But as we stood watching, we heard a sputtering sound like continuous gunfire and realized that the garrison

itself was on fire. "We'll be hit by bullets—it's too dangerous," shouted someone. The spectators scurried in all directions, but we stayed on, assuming that the fire had merely spread to the ammunition dump, and returned home around midnight.

Later in the night, I was awakened again. Guns were being fired, and people were running past the house shouting that war had broken out. Furuichi and I leapt out of bed, changed into our uniforms, and flew out of the house. Furuichi insisted that we go to school by way of Nakasaka to avoid stray bullets, but I ignored him and bounded straight up the slope at Kudan-zaka. It was extremely dangerous; bullets hissed past our heads and exploded in a shower of sparks on the stone fences of houses. By the time we reached Yasukuni Shrine, I was stumbling and gasping with every step. This was actually due to my beriberi, but I thought it had been brought on by fear and panic. I was so stricken with shame that I goaded myself to go on, but my legs simply refused to move. By good fortune, a two-passenger rickshaw was nearby. We jumped in and urged the man to hurry to the military academy.

The majority of the students had come at the first sign of an emergency and had already been deployed. Latecomers like ourselves—about twenty—were quickly organized into a unit, issued guns and ammunition, and ordered to catch up with the advance party. Led by Sergeant Major Egawa, we marched through Kudan and Hitotsubashi to the Army Ministry in Kajibashi and on to Sakuradamon. There we were told to take the route through Kōjimachi and report for guard duty at the Akasaka Palace. We linked up with the advance party just as the first rays of dawn were lighting the sky. Only then did we learn that the artillery unit of the Konoe Guards had mutinied.

The area around the palace was in utter chaos—soldiers and policemen running up and down the streets, local residents hauling tatami mats to barricade their houses. Order was restored on the twenty-fourth at about eight in the morning. Relieved of our duties, we returned to school. The mutiny apparently had been instigated by disgruntled elements who felt

that they had not been fairly compensated for their part in the war against Satsuma.* As to the underlying causes of the war itself—and the mutiny—one could probably trace them to the strains and stresses, the conflict of interests, the premature decisions and inconsistencies that were inherent in the Restoration.

The students assembled in the courtyard. "*Dismissed!*" My taut nerves suddenly gave way, and in a dead faint, I fell to the ground. When I regained consciousness, I was in bed in the infirmary. After two weeks of treatment, I was pronounced fully recovered.

I received a letter from Gosaburō in Aizu. "Father is in good health. You will be glad to know that, one by one, friends and acquaintances are returning to Aizu to help rebuild the land. It looks as though the upheavals of the Restoration are over for now, so I have decided to stay here in the land of our ancestors attending to Father and giving comfort to the spirits of our grandmother, mother, and sisters. You, Gorō, are to become a pillar of the new national army and restore the good name of Aizu." I finished the letter and folded my hands in prayer. Not long afterward, his health restored, my brother Shirō left for the United States to study.[16]

*About 260 noncommissioned soldiers took part in the mutiny known as the Takehashi Incident. The soldiers killed the battalion commander and fired on Finance Minister Ōkuma's residence. After a military tribunal, fifty-three were executed and the rest given various sentences.

Translator's Afterword

Shiba graduated from the Officers Academy in 1880. His advancement in the army was steady. He was assigned at various times to the General Staff and regimental duty, with periodic postings abroad—China, France, and England. He saw brief action in both the Sino-Japanese War (1894–1895) and the Russo-Japanese War (1904–1905). In 1913, he was made a lieutenant general and in 1919, a full general. He was put on the reserve list in 1923 and retired from the army in 1930.

Shiba achieved brief international fame in the summer of 1900 when, as "Colonel Shiba," he won the admiration and gratitude of the allied defenders of Peking during the Boxer Rebellion. That March, he had been assigned to the Japanese legation in Peking as military attaché; three months later, the legation quarters was attacked by thousands of antiforeign Boxer peasants and troops.

The siege lasted fifty-five days. According to Polly Smith, a young American who was caught in the siege, "The Japanese military attaché, Colonel Shiba, was by all odds the most respected of the various commanders on the scene. . . . He has done so splendidly . . . has proven such a general, that his opinion and help are asked by all the commanders."[1] Another eyewitness, Bertram Simpson, a member of Sir Robert Hart's custom staff, who had no kind words for the allied ministers and other officials, wrote the following in his memoirs:

They [the Japanese] have an extraordinary fellow in command, Colonel S——, the military attaché. He is awkward and stiff-legged, as are most Japanese, but he is very much in earnest, and already understands exactly what he can do and what he cannot do. . . . This little man, working quietly, is reducing things to order. . . . Already, I honor this man; soon I feel I shall be his slave.[2]

In describing the siege later on, George Morrison, special correspondent for *The Times* of London, wrote in his October 15 dispatch that "of all the nations represented at Peking, none had a task more arduous, or performed it more manfully than the Japanese." This, no doubt, owed a great deal to Shiba's leadership.

Shiba was decorated by his own country and by the eight allied nations that came under attack. His lectures on the siege were later published, together with reports by other Japanese participants, as *Pekin rōjō* (Tōyō bunko series no. 53, Heibonsha, 1965). During the siege, his thoughts, we imagine, turned to the last, desperate days of Aizu.

In late August 1996, guided by relatives of the Shiba family, I visited Shiba's grave at the Erinji Temple. As we climbed the steep hill behind the temple to the *chirr* of cicadas we could see the white walls of the restored castle through the foliage. The family grave was a single row of simple, gray stone markers, each bearing names now so familiar to me. The markers all faced the castle. The graves of the Aizu domain elders, I was told, were on a level higher. They, too, faced the castle.

Notes

Notes to the Introduction

1. The text of the house rules may be found in Hoshi Ryōichi, *Haisha no ishinshi: Arakawa Katsushige no nikki* (Tokyo: Chūō kōronsha, 1990), 2–3.

2. Aizu shidankai, ed., *Aizu sensō no subete* (Tokyo: Shin jinbutsu ōraisha, 1980), 39–40.

3. Yamaguchi Kōhei, ed., *Kinsei Aizushi no kenkyū* (Aizu-Wakamatsu: Rekishi shunjūsha, 1978), 1:410.

4. Conrad Totman, *The Collapse of the Tokugawa Bakufu, 1862–1868* (Honolulu: University of Hawai'i Press, 1980), 14. In another assessment, Katamori is described as "by no means mediocre as daimyo of that time went" (Iechika Yoshiki, *Bakumatsu seiji to tōbaku undō* [Tokyo: Yoshikawa kōbunkan, 1995], 26).

5. Hoshi, *Haisha no ishinshi*, 4.

6. As a reward for its actions, Aizu was granted the *bakufu* lands at Minamiyama in perpetuity. During his five-year tenure as Kyoto protector, Katamori would be granted additional moneys and revenues, eventually raising the Aizu holdings to 450,000 *koku* (Kodama Kōta and Kitajima Masamoto, eds., *Shinpen monogatari hanshi* [Tokyo: Shin jinbutsu ōraisha, 1976], 2:187), or according to another estimate, to 679,000 *koku* (*Aisu boshin senshi* [Tokyo: Aizu boshin senshi hensankai, 1993], 693). Despite this largess, the expenses eventually bankrupted the domain (Totman, *Collapse of the Tokugawa Bakufu*, 192).

7. Iechika, *Bakumatsu seiji to tōbaku undō*, 252–254. Iechika emphasizes that during the years from 1862 to 1865, Katamori was an equal-

ly important figure in Kyoto politics as Yoshinobu. Of the two, Kata-
mori took the hardest line: He protested the lenient terms of the first
punitive expedition against Chōshū and strongly favored continuing
the second expedition even after the initial setbacks to the *bakufu*
army. Iechika writes that many viewed the two expeditions as private
vendettas by Katamori against Chōshū.

8. Ernest Satow, *A Diplomat in Japan* (London: Oxford University Press,
 1968), 322.

9. Hayashi Gonsuke, *Waga shichijūnen o kataru* (Tokyo: Daiichi shobō,
 1935), 19. Hayashi's grandfather was also killed in the battle.

10. *Aizu boshin senshi*, 513.

11. Ibuka Kajinosuke, "Kaikoroku," in *Ibuka Kajinosuke to sono jidai*,
 vol. 1, ed. Ibuka Kajinosuke to sono jidai kankō iinkai (Tokyo: Meiji
 gakuin, 1969), 270–272. The youth also fretted that the Western-style
 uniform he had specially ordered would not be ready on time. To com-
 plete his outfit, he bought a pair of secondhand leather boots and cut
 off his samurai topknot to secure his French-style "shappo" on his
 head.

12. *Aizu boshin senshi*, 532–533.

13. Figures from this period are generally unreliable. Estimates range from
 more than ten thousand (Ishii Takashi, *Ishin no nairan* [Tokyo: Shi-
 seidō, 1968], 184) to thirty thousand (Sasaki Suguru, *Boshin sensō*
 [Tokyo: Chūō kōronsha, 1977], 159; *Bakumatsu ishin boshin sensō
 jiten* [Tokyo: Shin jinbutsu ōraisha, 1980], 296). William Willis, a
 British doctor who accompanied government troops to help the
 wounded, puts the figure at thirty thousand in one of his reports to the
 British legation (Hugh Cortazzi, *Dr. Willis in Japan: British Medical
 Pioneer, 1862–1877* [London and Dover, N.H.: The Athlone Press,
 1985], 158).

14. *Aizu boshin senshi*, 614

15. The casualties for other northeastern domains were: Sendai 829,
 Yonezawa 368, Nihonmatsu 336, Shōnai 320, and Nagaoka 310.
 Comparable losses on the government side were: Satsuma 514,
 Chōshū 427, and Tosa 106. Sources vary widely in their estimates; I
 have drawn on *Bakumatsu ishin boshin sensō jiten* (306) and Hirao
 Michio, *Boshin sensōshi* (Tokyo: Shin jinbutsu ōraisha, 1978), 217.
 The series of conflicts, beginning with the battle at Toba-Fushimi out-
 side Kyoto and ending with Enomoto's surrender in Hokkaido, is
 known as the Boshin War, after the fact that 1868 is the year of Boshin
 in the sexagenary cycle.

16. The figure usually given is 17,000, but this seems to have been inflat-
 ed to receive more aid from the government. According to one source,

it was closer to 12,000 (Onuma Atsushi, *Aizu no hōkai* [Tokyo: Nihon tosho kankōkai, 1990], 188). Another source puts it at 14,800 (Yamaguchi, *Kinsei Aizushi no kenkyū*, 2:160).

Notes to the Text

1. Before the reorganization in 1868, the Aizu military was divided into four battalions, each with varying numbers of subunits of four hundred men. Shiba's father was an officer in one such subunit, the Bangashiratai. His rank was approximately that of a company commander (Yamaguchi Kōhei, ed., *Aizu Nisshinkanshi* [Tokyo: Yoshikawa kōbunkan, 1983], 1:394; 2:370–372, 375).

2. Historians now agree that the edict was a forgery, written without imperial sanction by Iwakura Tomomi and other anti-*bakufu* nobles (Ishii Takashi, *Ishin no nairan* [Tokyo: Shiseidō, 1968], 11–17; Sasaki Suguru, "Taisei hōkan to tōbaku mitchoku," *Jinbun gahuhō* 80 [March 1997], 28–29).

3. On the day of the attack, Jūrō killed his mother, wife, daughter-in-law, and infant grandson, then set fire to the house and left for the castle. Though a son was killed in battle, he himself survived (*Aizu boshin senshi* [Tokyo: Aizu boshin senshi hensankai, 1933], 537).

4. In a memorandum dated January 23, 1869, Willis refers to the "bravery and energy" of the women in the castle: "They cut off their hair, busied themselves in preparing food, nursing the wounded and, in not a few instances, shouldered the rifle and bore a share in the fatigues of watching." Willis arrived in Wakamatsu in 1868/10 and treated seven hundred of the Aizu wounded, whom he found in a "deplorable state of filth and wretchedness." He also notes that troops were cruel on both sides (Hugh Cortazzi, *Dr. Willis in Japan: British Medical Pioneer, 1862–1877* [London and Dover, N.H.: The Athlone Press, 1985], 150–152). Matsumoto Jun, a doctor who studied in Nagasaki, also went to Aizu, with four of his students, to tend the wounded. Like Willis, he was shocked by the conditions and noted in his memoirs that not only did the Aizu people lack bandages but they washed wounds with *shōchū*, a low-grade distilled drink of high alcoholic content. Of the Aizu samurai he writes: "From the most senior to the lowliest in rank, they are uniformly competent, but they are narrow-minded and too intent on garnering individual honors. . . . They are nevertheless courageous and fearless in the face of death" (Matsumoto Jun, *Matsumoto Jun jiden*, Tōyō bunko series, no. 386 [Tokyo: Heibonsha, 1980], 70–72).

5. Tomekichi was actually given permission to use the fields and forests for a fee of twenty-five *ryō*, to be paid over twenty-five years. The

receipts for payment, in Shiba's hand, are in the possession of the Kanome family, still resident in Omokawasawa. I am grateful to Kanome Toyomi, Tomekichi's descendant, for showing them to me during a visit to Wakamatsu in 1996.

6. On the subject of the alienation of Aizu peasants from their former rulers, Willis, who witnessed Katamori's departure for Edo on 1868/10, writes of a "cold indifference" on the part of the commoners and "the general opinion" that the daimyo and his officials "had caused a cruel and unnecessary war and that in as much as they had failed to perform hara-kiri [ritual suicide] in the hour of defeat, they had forfeited all title to respect." Cortazzi, *Dr. Willis in Japan*, 153–154.

7. Writing in 1871, Ibuka mentions that a silver one-*bu* coin equaled one fourth of a *ryō* (Ibuka Kajinosuke, "Kaikoroku," in *Ibuka Kajinosuke to sono jidai*, vol. 1, ed. Ibuka Kajinosuke to sono jidai kankō iinkai [Tokyo: Meiji gakuin, 1969], 67).

8. I have been unable to find anyone who was at the Danish consulate at the time with a name remotely resembling the Japanese transcription. There was one Englishman, however, by the name of Thomas Wright Blakiston, who established a trading firm, Blakiston, Marr and Company, and was resident in Hakodate from 1861 to 1884. He may well have acted as an agent for the Danish consulate to purchase foreign rice for Tonami. Blakiston was involved in a legal case connected with his firm's issue of private paper currency, a practice prohibited by the Japanese government in 1872. The case was resolved in 1876, and if he is indeed the "Burikisuton" in Shiba's text, this may account for the undue length of Taichirō's own case, which was finally resolved that same year (Grace Fox, *Britain and Japan, 1858–1883* [Oxford: Clarendon Press, 1969], 348–349).

9. Hayashi Gonsuke, whose father and grandfather died at Toba-Fushimi, went to Tonami with his grandmother, mother, and sister (one baby sister died in the castle for lack of breast milk). He writes in his memoirs that "the conditions in Tonami were far worse than those during the siege," and that his family was obliged to sell half of their rice rations—less than three *gō* for the family of four—to buy miso, soy sauce, and other necessities (Hayashi Gonsuke, *Waga shichijūnen o kataru* [Tokyo: Daiichi shobō, 1935], 24).

10. Here, Shiba makes a distinction between *kinsatsu* (*dajōkansatsu*), the paper notes issued in 1868, and *shinshihei*, the notes made of superior German paper, which were issued in 1871 to counter the proliferation of counterfeit *kinsatsu*.

11. The peasant rebellion lasted two months. To quote Willis, the peasants "called for a new and just assessment of their land" and "sacked the

houses of the village mayors and in every instance burnt the land documents." Willis seems to have felt that the peasants were justified in their actions: "The poverty of the Aizu country was extreme. The houses were the poorest I have seen in any part of Japan, the farmers themselves were an ill-clad, undersized and weakly race. . . . There was a general feeling that Aizu [Katamori] had exceeded his strength both in men and money in maintaining such large forces at Kyoto as his office of protector of the Mikado had entailed upon him for the last six years. . . . I have heard Japanese of intelligence say that if Aizu and his advisers received a free pardon, it would be impossible to force them again upon the people of their province" (Cortazzi, *Dr. Willis in Japan*, 155–156).

12. Nagaoka Hisashige (1841–1877) served in the Tonami government and at the time of the narrative had come to Tokyo and become friendly with Itagaki Taisuke. He started a newspaper that was critical of the government and, in 1876, was accused of fomenting an antigovernment plot and was sentenced to jail, where he died of illness.

13. In 1871, Yamakawa Sutematsu (1860–1919), along with Tsuda Umeko and three other girls, was chosen by the government to study in the United States. The twelve-year-old Sutematsu stayed for ten years, graduated from Vassar College, and on her return married Ōyama Iwao, a Satsuma general who served in the Boshin War.

14. The Army Cadet School had its origins in a school founded in Osaka in 1868 to train future army officers. The school was later merged with a French-language school in Yokohama and officially opened in Tokyo as the Rikugun Yōnen Seitotai in 1871. It was renamed the Rikugun Yōnen Gakkō in 1873.

15. The redoubtable Sagawa "Ogre" Kanbei also fought in Kyushu as the head of a police unit made up of 150 former Aizu samurai. To the end, he refused to use a modern weapon and was shot and killed at Mount Aso.

16. Shirō (1852–1922), better known by his pen name, Tōkai Sanshi, went to the United States with the financial help of the Iwasaki family, the founders of Mitsubishi. He remained there for seven years, studying briefly at Harvard and earning a bachelor of finance degree from the University of Pennsylvania. During this time, he became interested in independence movements and began writing *Kajin no kigū*. The first installment was published after his return to Japan in 1885. The novel describes the chance meeting at Independence Hall in Philadelphia of a Japanese youth with two young women—one, an aristocratic exile from Spain, the other, a fervid supporter of the Irish independence movement—and his subsequent quest to win the hand of the first. The plot is convoluted (there were eventually eight installments), with many digressions, such as encounters with Kossuth and

Parnell's younger sister. Although it is no longer much read, the book at the time appealed to the idealism of young Japanese and sold in the tens of thousands. A Chinese translation was also made. It is interesting to note that in telling the story of the protagonist's early years, the author drew on his own experiences on the day of the enemy attack on Wakamatsu.

Notes to the Translator's Afterword

1. As quoted in Richard O'Connor, *The Spirit Soldiers: A Historical Narrative of the Boxer Rebellion* (New York: G. P. Putnam, 1973), 197.

2. Bertram Simpson, *Indiscreet Letters from Peking* (New York: Dodd Mead, 1909), 114.

Bibliography

Adachi Yoshio. *Aizu Tonami ōrai.* Aizu-Wakamatsu: Rekishi shunjūsha, 1989.

Aizu boshin senshi. Tokyo: Aizu boshin senshi hensankai, 1933.

Aizu shidankai, ed. *Aizu sensō no subete.* Tokyo: Shin jinbutsu ōraisha, 1980.

Anzai Sōji. *Fukushima no boshin sensō.* Aizu-Wakamatsu: Rekishi shunjūsha, 1981.

Asakura Haruhiko, ed. *Meiji kansei jiten.* Tokyo: Tōkyōdō shuppan, 1969.

Cortazzi, Hugh. *Dr. Willis in Japan: British Medical Pioneer, 1862–1877.* London and Dover, N.H.: The Athlone Press, 1985.

Craig, Albert M. *Chōshū in the Meiji Restoration.* Cambridge: Harvard University Press, 1961.

Fairbank, John K., Edwin O. Reischauer, and Albert M. Craig. *East Asia, The Modern Transformation.* Boston: Houghton Mifflin, 1965.

Fox, Grace. *Britain and Japan, 1858–1883.* Oxford: Clarendon Press, 1969.

Haraguchi Kiyoshi. *Boshin sensō.* Tokyo: Hanawa shobō, 1963.

Hata Ikuhiko, ed. *Nihon rikugun sōgō jiten.* Tokyo: Tōkyō daigaku shuppankai, 1991.

Hayashi Gonsuke. *Waga shichijūnen o kataru.* Tokyo: Daiichi shobō, 1935.

Hirao Michio. *Boshin sensōshi.* Tokyo: Shin jinbutsu ōraisha, 1978.

Hoshi Ryōichi. *Haisha no ishinshi: Arakawa Katsushige no nikki.* Tokyo: Chūō kōronsha, 1990.

Ibuka Kajinosuke. "Kaikoroku." In *Ibuka Kajinosuke to sono jidai.* Vol. 1. Edited by Ibuka Kajinosuke to sono jidai kankō iinkai. Tokyo: Meiji gakuin, 1969.

Iechika Yoshiki. *Bakumatsu seiji to tōbaku undō.* Tokyo: Yoshikawa kōbunkan, 1995.

Ishii Takashi. *Ishin no nairan*. Tokyo: Shiseidō, 1968.

Jiji tsūshinsha, ed. *Aizu jinbutsu bunken mokuroku*. Tokyo: Jiji tsūshinsha, 1914.

Kamiya Jirō and Soda Kōichi, eds. *Bakumatsu ishin sanbyaku han sōran*. Tokyo: Shin jinbutsu ōraisha, 1977.

Kodama Kōta and Kitajima Masamoto, eds. *Shinpen monogatari hanshi*. Vol. 2. Tokyo: Shin jinbutsu ōraisha, 1976.

Konishi Shirō et. al., eds. *Bakumatsu ishin jiten*. Tokyo: Shin jinbutsu ōraisha, 1983.

Matsumoto Jun. *Matsumoto Jun jiden*. Tōyō bunko series, no. 386. Tokyo: Heibonsha, 1980.

Matsushita Yoshio. *Meiji gunseishi*. Tokyo: Ikuseisha, 1938.

Miyamoto Mataji et. al., eds. *Kinsei Osaka no bukka to rishi*. Tokyo: Sōbunsha, 1963.

Miyazaki Tomihachi, ed. *Monogatari Aizu sensō hiwa*. Tokyo: Shin jinbutsu ōraisha, 1988.

Nagaoka Keinosuke. *Aizu-han e no banka*. Tokyo: Erumu kabushiki kaisha, 1975.

Nakamura Akihiko. *Hoshina Masayuki*. Tokyo: Chūō kōronsha, 1995.

O'Connor, Richard. *The Spirit Soldiers: A Historical Narrative of the Boxer Rebellion*. New York: G. P. Putnam, 1973.

Onuma Atsushi. *Aizu no hōkai*. Tokyo: Nihon tosho kankōkai, 1990.

Ōta Toshiho, ed. *Bakumatsu ishin boshin sensō jiten*. Tokyo: Shin jinbutsu ōraisha, 1980.

Sasaki Suguru. *Boshin sensō*. Tokyo: Chūō kōronsha, 1977.

———. "Taisei hōkan to tōbaku mitchoku." *Jinbun gakuhō* 80 (March 1997): 1–32.

Satow, Ernest. *A Diplomat in Japan*. London: Oxford University Press, 1968.

Shiba Shirō [Tōkai Sanshi]. *Kajin no kigū*. Reprint. Tokyo: Jiji tsūshinsha, 1970.

Simpson, Bertram [B. L. Putnam Weale]. *Indiscreet Letters from Peking*. New York: Dodd Mead, 1909.

Totman, Conrad. *The Collapse of the Tokugawa Bakufu, 1862–1868*. Honolulu: University of Hawai'i Press, 1980.

Yamaguchi Kōhei, ed. *Aizu Nisshinkanshi*. Tokyo: Yoshikawa kōbunkan, 1983.

———. *Kinsei Aizushi no kenkyū*. 2 vols. Aizu-Wakamatsu: Rekishi shunjūsha, 1978.

Yanatori Sangi. *Aizu Tsurugajō*. Tokyo: Shin jinbutsu ōraisha, 1974.

About the Translator

Teruko Craig is senior lecturer emerita in Japanese at Tufts University and is currently an associate in research at the Reischauer Institute of Japanese Studies at Harvard University. Her previous book-length translations are *Misui's Story: The Autobiography of a Tokugawa Samurai* (University of Arizona Press, 1988; paperback edition, 1991) and *The Autobiography of Shibusawa Eiichi: From Peasant to Entrepreneur* (University of Tokyo Press, 1994).

CPSIA information can be obtained
at www.ICGtesting.com
Printed in the USA
FSOW01n1116150816
23745FS